Self-Esteem

Encouraging Self and Others

Eddie Jane Pelkey and Irene Getz

Augsburg Fortress, Minneapolis

Contents

Introduction	3
Series introduction	5
1 Loving and Being Loved	11
2 Knowing and Accepting Myself	19
3 Families and Friends	27
4 The Wider World of Relationships	35
5 The Matter of Appearance	43
6 Confidently on Our Way	52
Facilitator Helps	61
Appendix	72
Group directory	72
Group commitments	73
Prayer requests	74
Prayers	74
Resources	75
Response form	79

INTERSECTIONS
Small Group Series

Self-Esteem
Encouraging Self and Others

Developed in cooperation with the Division for Congregational Ministries

George W. Johnson, series introduction
Andrea Lee Schieber and William Congdon, editors
The Wells Group, series design
Daniel R. Burow, cover photo

Scripture quotations are from New Revised Standard Version Bible, copyright 1989 Division of Christian Education of the National Council of the Churches of Christ in the United States of America. Used by permission.

Copyright © 1995 Augsburg Fortress
All rights reserved. May not be reproduced.
ISBN 0-8066-0137-X
Printed on 50% recycled paper (10% postconsumer fibers)
Manufactured in U.S.A.

1 2 3 4 5 6 7 8 9 0 1 2 3 4 5 6 7 8 9

Introduction

What is self-esteem?

Self-esteem is the ability to appreciate our own worth and importance, while at the same time being accountable for ourselves and acting responsibly toward others. Each of us has some moments of self-doubt because we have encountered times when our worth was questioned.

Purpose of this group

The purposes of this support and recovery group on self-esteem are to help the participants:

- increase their self-esteem;
- understand the biblical basis for self-love and for thinking positively about themselves;
- find answers about the sources of their self-esteem;
- discover more about who they are, their qualities, abilities, interests, and values;
- build on what is good, work on what is not so good, and to be able to accept themselves realistically;
- use their abilities and insights to reach out to others.

Contents of the course

This course begins by looking at biblical passages about loving ourselves (Luke 10:25-28), moves into the larger circles of families, friends, and ministry to others, then comes back to ourselves with our dreams and goals.

The six themes of this study are as follows:

1. "Loving and Being Loved." Self-esteem is rooted in who we are, children of God.

2. "Knowing and Accepting Ourselves." How we perceive ourselves affects our self-esteem.

3. "Families and Friends." Our closest relationships greatly affect how we think about ourselves.

4. "The Wider World of Relationships." Our workplace and other social contacts also influence our attitudes about ourselves.

5. "The Matter of Appearance." How we look, and especially changes in how we look, impact our self-esteem.

6. "Confidence to Move Ahead." To have good self-esteem, we need to know how to love, keep our lives in balance, and have dreams for the future.

Benefits of group interaction

A key for a group on self-esteem is the interaction among group members. Our self-esteem has its roots in what our parents and other adults mirrored to us about our worth. Even though we can do some work alone, we continue to need other people to affirm us and to let us know that they think we are all right. The group interactions will be crucial to the success of this group.

The ability to state viewpoints and to hear what others say offers a real opportunity for personal growth. Others with differing viewpoints may disturb us at first, but we can learn to agree and disagree in an environment of mutual trust and support. The basic foundation of all group interaction will be the common bond of wanting to help ourselves and others grow in self-esteem.

The materials in this book are related to life situations, past and present, and assist us to examine various ways we can apply the knowledge we gain to our lives.

Spiritual foundations

The Christian faith teaches us that we are not alone as we try to change unworkable aspects of our lives and to strengthen what is good. God is the one who heals, whose will is that each of us have an abundant life. The relation of self-esteem to our spiritual lives is discussed in virtually every session. Knowing that God created us, redeemed us, and continues to love and guide us is the best foundation we can have. This group has the potential of being a deeply meaningful and spiritual experience.

Introducing the series

Welcome into the family of those who are part of small groups! Intersections Small Group Series will help you and other members of your group build relationships and discover ways to connect the Christian faith with your everyday life.

This book is prepared for those who want to make a difference in this world, who want to grow in their Christian faith, as well as for those who are beginning to explore the Christian faith. The information in this introduction to the Intersections small group experience can help your group make the most out of your time together.

Biblical encouragement

"Do not be conformed to this world, but be transformed by the renewing of your minds, so that you may discern what is the will of God—what is good and acceptable and perfect" (Romans 12:2).

Small groups provide an atmosphere where the Holy Spirit can transform lives. As you share your life stories and learn together, God's Spirit can work to enlighten and direct you.

Strength is provided to face the pressures to conform to forces and influences that are opposed to what is "good and acceptable and perfect." To "be transformed" is an ongoing experience of God's grace as we take up the cross and follow Jesus. Changed lives happen as we live in community with one another. Small groups encourage such change and growth.

What is a small group?

A number of definitions and descriptions of the small group ministry experience exist throughout the church. Roberta Hestenes, a Presbyterian pastor and author, defines a small group as an intentional face-to-face gathering of three to twelve people who meet regularly with the common purpose of discovering and growing in the possibilities of the abundant life.

Whatever definition you use, the following characteristics are important.

Small—Seven to ten people is ideal so that everyone can be heard and no one's voice is lost. More than twelve members makes genuine caring difficult.

Intentional—Commitment to the group is a high priority.

Personal—Sharing experiences and insights is more important than mastering content.

Conversational—Leaders that facilitate conversation, rather than teach, are the key to encouraging participation.

Friendly—Having a warm, accepting, nonjudgmental atmosphere is essential.

Christ-centered—The small group experience is biblically based, related to the real world, and founded on Christ.

Features of Intersections Small Group Series

A small group model

A number of small group ministry models exist. Most models include three types of small groups:

- *Discipleship groups*—where people gather to grow in Christian faith and life;
- *Support and recovery groups*—which focus on special interests, concerns, or needs; and
- *Ministry groups*—which have a task-oriented focus.

Intersections Small Group Series presently offers material for discipleship groups and support and recovery groups.

For discipleship groups, this series offers a variety of courses with Bible study at the center. What makes a discipleship group different from traditional group Bible studies? In discipleship groups, members bring their life experience to the exploration of the biblical material.

For support and recovery groups, Intersections Small Group Series offers topical material to assist group members in dealing with issues related to their common experience, hurt, or interest. An extra section of facilitator helps in the back of the book will assist leaders of support and recovery groups to anticipate and prepare for special circumstances and needs that may arise as group members explore a topic.

Ministry groups can benefit from an environment that includes prayer, biblical reflection, and relationship building, in addition to their task focus.

Four essentials

Prayer, personal sharing, biblical reflection, and a group ministry task are part of each time you gather. These are all important for Christian community to be experienced. Each of the six chapter themes in each book includes:

- Short prayers to open and close your time together.
- Carefully worded questions to make personal sharing safe, nonthreatening, and voluntary.
- A biblical base from which to understand and discover the power and grace of God. God's Word is the compass that keeps the group on course.
- A group ministry task to encourage both individuals and the group as a whole to find ways to put faith into action.

Flexibility

Each book contains six chapter themes that may be covered in six sessions or easily extended for groups that meet for a longer period of time. Each chapter theme is organized around two to three main topics with supplemental material to make it easily adaptable to your small group's needs. You need not use all the material. Most themes will work well for 1½- to 2-hour sessions, but a variety of scheduling options is possible.

Bible based

Each of the six chapter themes in the book includes one or more Bible texts printed in its entirety from the New Revised Standard Version of the Bible. This makes it easy for all group members to read and learn from the same text. Participants will be encouraged through questions, with exercises, and by other group members to address biblical texts in the context of their own lives.

User friendly

The material is prepared in such a way that it is easy to follow, practical, and does not require a professional to lead it. Designating one to be the facilitator to guide the group is important, but there is no requirement for this person to be theologically trained or an expert in the course topic. Many times options are given so that no one will feel forced into any set way of responding. The "Facilitator Helps" on pages 61-71 explain ways to adapt the material to the interests and needs of the group.

Group goals and process

1. Creating a group covenant or contract for your time together will be important. During your first meeting, discuss these important characteristics of all small groups and decide how your group will handle them.

Confidentiality—Agreeing that sensitive issues that are shared remain in the group.

Regular attendance—Agreeing to make meetings a top priority.

Nonjudgmental behavior—Agreeing to confess one's own shortcomings, if appropriate, not those of others, and not giving advice unless asked for it.

Prayer and support—Being sensitive to one another, listening, becoming a caring community.

Accountability—Being responsible to each other and open to change.

Items in your covenant should be agreed upon by all members. Add to the group covenant as you go along. Space to record key aspects is included in the back of this book. See page 73.

2. Everyone is responsible for the success of the group, but do arrange to have one facilitator who can guide the group process each time you meet.

The facilitator is not a teacher or healer. Teaching, learning, and healing happen from the group experience. The facilitator is more of a shepherd who leads the flock to where they can feed and drink and feel safe.

Remember, an important goal is to experience genuine love and community in a Christ-centered atmosphere. To help make this happen, the facilitator encourages active listening and honest sharing. This person allows the material to facilitate opportunities for self-awareness and interaction with others.

Leadership is shared in a healthy group, but the facilitator is the one designated to set the pace, keep the group focused, and enable the members to support and care for each other.

People need to sense trust and freedom as the group develops; therefore, avoid "shoulds" or "musts" in your group.

3. Taking on a group ministry task can help members of your group balance personal growth with service to others.

In your first session, identify ways your group can offer help to others within the church or in your surrounding community. Take time at each meeting to do or arrange for that ministry task. Many times it is in the doing that we discover what we believe or how God is working in our lives.

4. Starting or continuing a personal action plan offers a way to address personal needs that you become aware of in your small group experience.

For example, you might want to spend more time in conversation with a friend or spouse. Your action plan might state, "I plan to visit with Terry two times before our next small group meeting."

If you decide to pursue a personal action plan, consider sharing it with your small group. Your group can be helpful in at least three ways: by giving support; helping to define the plan in realistic, measurable ways; and offering a source to whom you can be accountable.

5. Prayer is part of small group fellowship. There is great power in group prayer, but not everyone feels free to offer spontaneous prayer. That's okay.

Learning to pray aloud takes time and practice. If you feel uncomfortable, start with simple and short prayers. And remember to pray for other members between sessions.

Use page 74 in the back of this book to note prayer requests made by group members.

6. Consider using a journal to help reflect on your experiences and insights between meeting times.

Writing about feelings, ideas, and questions can be one way to express yourself; plus it helps you remember what so often gets lost with time.

The "Daily Walk" component includes material that can get your journaling started. This, of course, is up to you and need not be done on any regular schedule. Even doing it once a week can be time well spent.

How to use this book

The material provided for each session is organized around some key components. If you are the facilitator for your small group, be sure to read this section carefully.

NOTE: Those who plan (or might plan) to lead this small group should read the "Facilitator Helps" starting on page 61.

The facilitator's role is to establish a hospitable atmosphere and set a tone that encourages participants to share, reflect, and listen to each other. Some important practical things can help make this happen.

- ◼ Whenever possible meet in homes. Be sure to provide clear directions about how to get there.
- ◼ Use name tags for several sessions.
- ◼ Place the chairs in a circle and close enough for everyone to hear and feel connected.
- ◼ Be sure everyone has access to a book; preparation will pay off.

Welcoming

For a course on self-esteem, choose bright, cheerful visuals—banners, streamers, large photos of happy people. As people enter, you might want to have music playing, perhaps light classical music such as Vivaldi's "Four Seasons."

Name tags help members get to know each other. Have them write their names in large print using dark markers. Colors, drawings, and symbols can be added.

Ask for ideas from group members to make your meeting room a welcoming place. This will encourage creativity and help everyone to feel comfortable and at home.

If refreshments are to be served, determine at the first session if these will be furnished on a rotating basis or how they will be supplied.

Focus

Each of the six chapter themes in this book has a brief focus statement. Read it aloud. It will give everyone a sense of the direction for each session and provide some boundaries so that people will not feel lost or frustrated trying to cover everything. The focus also connects the theme to the course topic.

Community building

This opening activity is crucial to a relaxed, friendly atmosphere. It will prepare the ground for gradual group development. Two "Community Building" options are provided under each theme. With the facilitator giving his or her response to the questions first, others are free to follow.

One purpose for this section is to allow everyone to participate as he or she responds to nonthreatening questions. The activity serves as a check-in time when participants are invited to share how things are going or what is new.

Make this time light and fun; remember, humor is a welcome gift. Use fifteen to twenty minutes for this activity in your first few sessions and keep the entire group together.

During your first meeting, encourage group members to write down names and phone numbers (when appropriate) of the other members, so people can keep in touch. Use page 75 for this purpose.

Discovery

This component focuses on exploring the theme for your time together, using material that is read, and questions and exercises that encourage sharing of personal insights and experiences.

Reading material includes a Bible text with commentary written by the topic writer. Have volunteers read the Bible texts aloud. Read the commentary aloud only when it seems helpful. The main passage to be used is printed so that everyone operates from a common translation and sees the text.

"A Further Look" is included in some places to give you additional study material if time permits. Use it to explore related passages and questions. Be sure to have your own Bible handy.

Questions and exercises related to the theme will invite personal sharing and storytelling. Keep in mind that as you listen to each other's stories, you are inspired to live more fully in the grace and will of God. Such exchanges make Christianity relevant and transformation more likely to happen. Caring relationships are key to clarifying one's beliefs. Sharing personal experiences and insights is what makes the small group spiritually satisfying.

Most people are open to sharing their life stories, especially if they're given permission to do so and they know someone will actively listen. Starting with the facilitator's response usually works best. On some occasions you may want to break the group into units of three or four persons to explore certain questions. When you reconvene, relate your experience to the whole group. The phrase "Explore and Relate," which appears occasionally in the margin, refers to this recommendation. Encourage couples to separate for this smaller group activity. Appoint someone to start the discussion.

Wrap-up

Plan your schedule so that there will be enough time for wrapping up. This time can include work on your group ministry task, review of key discoveries during your time together, identifying personal and prayer concerns, closing prayers, and the Lord's Prayer.

The facilitator can help the group identify and plan its ministry task. Introduce the idea and decide on your group ministry task during "Wrap-up" time in the first session. Tasks need not be grandiose. Activities might include:

- Ministry in your community, such as "adopting" a food shelf, clothes closet, or homeless shelter; sponsoring equipment, food, or clothing drives; or sending members to staff the shelter.

- Ministry to members of the church, such as writing notes to those who are ill or bereaved.

- Church tasks where volunteers are always needed, such as serving refreshments during the fellowship time after worship, stuffing envelopes for a mailing, or taking responsibility for altar preparations for one month.

Depending upon the task, you can use part of each meeting time to carry out or plan the task.

In the "Wrap-up," allow time for people to share insights and encouragements and to voice special prayer requests. Just to mention someone who needs prayer is a form of prayer. The "Wrap-up" time may include a brief worship experience with candles, prayers, and singing. You might form a circle and hold hands. Silence can be effective. If you use the Lord's Prayer in your group, select the version that is known in your setting. There is space on page 74 to record the version your group uses. Another closing prayer is also printed on page 74. Before you go, ask members to pray for one another during the week. Remember also any special concerns or prayer requests.

Daily walk

Seven Bible readings and a thought, prayer, and verse for the journey related to the material just discussed are provided for those who want to keep the theme before them between sessions. These brief readings may be used for devotional time. Some group members may want to memorize selected passages. The Bible readings can also be used for supplemental study by the group if needed. Prayer for other group members can also be part of this time of personal reflection.

A word of encouragement

No material is ever complete or perfect for every situation or group. Creativity and imagination will be important gifts for the facilitator to bring to each theme. Keep in mind that it is in community that we are challenged to grow in Jesus Christ. Together we become what we could not become alone. It is God's plan that it be so.

For additional resources and ideas see *Starting Small Groups—and Keeping Them Going* (Minneapolis: Augsburg Fortress, 1995).

1 Loving and Being Loved

Focus

To increase our self-esteem, we need to know that we are worth loving, to unlearn the negative messages we were taught, and to learn new and healthier ways to think.

Community building

Option

Complete these two sentences: 1) One thing I do not like about myself is.... 2) One thing I like about myself is.... Introduce yourself to other group members, using those two sentences as a beginning.

Make a name tag for yourself. Write your first name and add a drawing or words that describe something about you. For example, someone may draw stick figures who are dancing or add the words "I love to dance." Your words and pictures can be humorous, serious, or anything in between. Introduce yourself to other group members, using what you put on your name tags as a beginning.

Then take the time to write down two or three of your initial hopes for your experience in this small group. Also think about some goals for the group or possible group outcomes and write them down on page 73. Identifying outcomes will help your group to have a common agenda as well as individual ones.

Opening prayer

Dear Lord, help us as we think about who we are. Your presence helps us to have the courage to share ourselves with each other as we come to know and appreciate ourselves and others more fully. Amen.

Discovery 1

Loving and accepting myself

Read aloud.

Who am I? Am I able to accept who I am? These two questions can lead to thought-provoking conversations as we begin to explore self-esteem.

First we need some definitions. Self-esteem has been described as a favorable appreciation of oneself, the ability to care about and love oneself. In 1990, the California Task Force to Promote Self-Esteem and Personal and Social Responsibility defined self-esteem as "appreciating my own worth and importance and having the character to be accountable for myself and to act responsibly toward others." That definition's emphasis on accountability and responsible action toward others is worth noting, and is an emphasis that will be followed in this study.

Adapted from *Developing Self-Esteem*, by Connie Palladino, copyright © 1989 Crisp Publications. Reprinted by permission.

The definitions sound fine, but we may ask how to keep such attention to ourselves from going too far. The world seems to have too many arrogant, self-centered people in it already. How can a small group on self-esteem avoid extremes? A first step is to see what the Bible says.

Read aloud and discuss.

Luke 10:25-28

25Just then a lawyer stood up to test Jesus. "Teacher," he said, "what must I do to inherit eternal life?" 26He said to him, "What is written in the law? What do you read there?" 27He answered, "You shall love the Lord your God with all your heart, and with all your soul, and with all your strength, and with all your mind; and your neighbor as yourself." 28And he said to him, "You have given the right answer; do this, and you will live."

Jesus gave us two anchors to be sure we don't get too preoccupied with ourselves. First, we are to love God with everything we have—a joyful, self-transcending love. Second, we are to be compassionate. Jesus' statement assumes that we will love ourselves and says that we are to love our neighbor with the same kind of caring concern that we have for ourselves. The three loves—love of God, love of self, and love of neighbor—are closely bound together. Sometimes we forget that love of self is an appropriate and necessary kind of love.

Explore and relate.
Explore in groups of three or four; then *relate* a brief summary to the entire group.

Consider this

"Self-love and self-preservation are the ground of our humanity. If we lack an inner relationship of self-love, our outer love becomes an obsessive search for self-validation. Spiritual masters from the beginning of time have taught us this. It is a foundation of Jesus' teaching."

John Bradshaw, *Creating Love*, page 266.

Read and discuss as a group.

We need to be aware that God's love for us has a broader basis than our accomplishments. We are loved for who we are. We would be loved if we were totally paralyzed and unable to do a thing. We are loved for our "being" and not just for our "doing." Our own acceptance of ourselves also needs to be based on our "selves," our being, and not only on what we do.

Sometimes when we feel inadequate and are trying to convince ourselves that we are acceptable, we need to remember that God's answer that we are fully loved has been there all the time. God loves us just as we are.

- At what times in your life were you not really able to love yourself much? Who or what helped you?
- The Bible tells us God loves us and is close at hand for us, not far away and uncaring. How has your faith helped you?

A further look

Read and discuss as a group.

In John 3:16, we read that "God so loved the world that he gave his only Son." God did not send Jesus to a people without merit, but rather to a people whom God loved. Our faith teaches us that God loves us, cherishes us, and believes we are important.

- What does this verse teach us about God? About ourselves? *God C/s us enough to give His 1 t only son*
- How do those teachings affect our feelings of self-esteem? *That someone C/s me enough to die 4 me.* *I am being loved.*

Discovery 2

Where it all began

Read and discuss.

How we think and feel about ourselves begins in our infancy. When a baby needs something and its parents or caregivers fill the need promptly, the infant begins to establish a sense of trust. With trust and anticipation that its needs will be met, the baby soon begins to connect the response with positive feelings about itself. A belief system about its worth is being established.

Some babies and young children may not be so fortunate. For whatever reasons, their parents or caregivers do not meet their needs adequately, and the children's sense of trust and positive feelings about themselves suffer.

As we move through childhood, adolescence, young adulthood, and adulthood, some of our early learnings stay with us. Some may nourish us but others disable us. The adults around us during our childhood "mirror" to us who we are, how valuable we are. If we hear them saying negative things about us, abusing us, ignoring us, or shaming us a lot, we will incorporate those messages and feelings. As children, we have no way to know if they were right or wrong in their evaluation of us.

Read through this list, checking the items that were to some extent true for you. After completing this, meet in small groups to talk about your experiences.

■ My parents or others said or implied I should have been:

____ Strong and athletic

____ Musical (or otherwise talented)

____ Smarter, perhaps a straight-A student

____ A boy (or girl)

____ Prettier or more handsome, less plain

____ Confident and able to perform well

____ More obedient and hard-working

____ Less noisy, messy, and wild

____ Like my brother(s) or sister(s)

____ Thinner (or heavier)

____ Other (_____)

Read aloud and discuss.

Our self-esteem has suffered from the many negatives we have heard and experienced. However, for nearly everyone childhood also holds some good memories. Let's also take some time to think of some good experiences.

All through our lives, we have established benchmarks of success. As infants, we learned to hold a bottle successfully; as small children, we tied our shoes and learned to read and write; as adolescents, we learned new social skills and how to interact with many people; and as adults, we learned to negotiate to meet our needs. All these learning experiences helped to build our self-esteem.

- Identify times in your life when you learned or accomplished something and mastered new skills.
- How did you feel about yourself and your abilities?
- Did you learn self-reliance?
- Did you also learn how to ask for help when you needed it?

In groups of three or four, tell each other first about your accomplishments and then about people who were there for you.

A second source of positive memories is the people who somehow helped us feel a little better about ourselves: perhaps a loving grandparent, a teacher, a friend, or a neighbor.

- Identify some loving, affirming people who helped counteract some of the negatives you experienced as a child.
- What did these people do and say that helped you feel better about yourself?

Discovery 3

Nourishing our self-esteem

Read aloud.

Take a look at yourself. Sometime you may want to study yourself in a mirror, but for now just lean back in your chair and study your hand. Think about all the many tasks your hand performs for you. If it is the hand you write with, then think about the knowledge your body has that allows this hand to function. Consider what a marvelous instrument your hand is. You would have a hard time functioning without it.

Many times we take ourselves for granted and underestimate how fearfully and wonderfully we are created. For our hands to work, they need a supply of nourishment; they need electrical impulses from our brains; and they need to be protected from danger.

Self-esteem can be compared to our hands. We may hardly think of it and often take it for granted. Yet self-esteem too needs nourishment and positive messages.

To build self-esteem, we must be good to ourselves and be patient with ourselves. We need to recognize what needs to be changed and what we are able to change, as well as what we cannot change. The Serenity Prayer of Alcoholics Anonymous says, "God, grant me the serenity to accept the things I cannot change, the courage to change the things I can, and the wisdom to know the difference."

Sometimes we wish we could change something that is not possible for us to change, such as our past experience, our height, a chronic illness we may have, our nationality, or our race. The first part of our task here is to accept them. The next step is to identify changes that would be possible and beneficial.

It is essential to take this journey one step at a time. Members of Alcoholics Anonymous say, "Easy does it." Those are good words to remember when we are rebuilding our damaged self-esteem.

Self-esteem is related to and part of our self-definition. Earnie Larsen, a workshop leader and author who applies Alcoholics Anonymous' Twelve Steps to many kinds of problems, says that we need to remember that we cannot outperform our own self-definition. So what can we do if we define ourselves in negative ways? We can work on changing it.

Suggestions

Enjoying humor, laughter, and fun things; being with healthy, uplifting people; nourishing spiritual life with quiet time; writing in a journal, Bible reading, other reading, and prayer; choosing experiences that help you heal and grow.

One effective technique Larsen describes is "stop-start" actions. As people stop negative behaviors (such as procrastination, staying home even when invited out, eating too much, keeping problems to themselves), they start to feel better about themselves. As they start taking positive actions (calling a friend, getting the bills paid, going to an enjoyable movie, getting a haircut), their self-esteem grows even more.

In the space below, write down three actions that detract from your good feelings about yourself and that you might consider stopping. Then write down three actions that would make you feel good about yourself and that you could start doing. (Some suggestions for healthy behaviors are listed in the margin.) Finally, discuss the questions that follow.

- In small groups, discuss what you have written.

- Choose one "stop behavior" and one "start behavior" that you are quite sure you will be able to do. Next week you will either report on your success or revise your choices if they didn't work too well.

Part of our journey is to keep turning to God in prayer, offering thanks for acceptance and love, and asking for guidance. Prayer helps us be more open to new thoughts, ideas, and actions.

We need to allow ourselves to be the fallible human beings that we are, yet knowing that God accepts us. With God's help we have the ability to begin making some changes. Our self-esteem will increase as we claim God's great love for us and as we are able to accept and love ourselves.

A further look

Read 1 John 3:1a. Because of God's great love, we are called the children of God. Each of us was created as a unique individual.

- What makes you unique?
- When have your special qualities made you feel good about yourself?

Wrap-up

See page 10 in the introduction for a description of "Wrap-up."

Ongoing prayer requests can be listed on page 74. See page 74 for suggested closing prayers.

Before you go, take time for the following:

- Group ministry task

- Review

- Personal concerns and prayer concerns

- Closing prayers

Daily walk

Bible readings

Day 1
Isaiah 43:1-7

Day 2
Matthew 6:25-33

Day 3
Ephesians 4:11-16

Day 4
Psalm 37:3-7

Day 5
Isaiah 40:28-31

Day 6
Matthew 7:7-11

Day 7
Psalm 119:89-94

Thought for the journey

I will begin to dismantle old, negative thoughts and actions and start working on uplifting thoughts and actions. I will remind myself of the many positive things that I do in my everyday life.

Prayer for the journey

God, be with me as I journey on a path of self-discovery. Give me insights into any stumbling blocks to self-acceptance and self-esteem. Help me to let go of unhealthy expectations of myself. Amen.

Verse for the journey

"We love because he first loved us" (1 John 4:19).

2 Knowing and Accepting Myself

Focus

Understanding who we are is a first step in increasing our self-esteem. Knowing and accepting ourselves can have an enormous impact on how we live our lives and how we relate to other people.

Community building

Option

Develop a brief commercial about yourself, perhaps "selling" yourself to a possible employer. List six wonderful attributes about yourself (kind, friendly, nice smile, and so forth). Listeners can add more as each person speaks.

Begin with a period of relaxation. Close your eyes and imagine a place that is important to you (perhaps your present home or childhood home, or a vacation spot). Write down a brief description of your place. Then tell what is special about the place and how it is related to your self-esteem.

Afterwards, if you are willing, tell the group about your special place. Notice if any of the places described have something in common, such as the person felt good to be there or it was fun, comforting, or beautiful.

Then, take a few minutes to report to your small group about your "start-stop" actions from last time. Applaud those who did what they said and encourage the others.

Opening prayer

Lord, you know us from the tops of our heads to the soles of our feet. Help us to value ourselves in the same way that you value us, holding us in high esteem and love. Lead us as we learn to know ourselves better. Amen.

Discovery 1

Genesis 1:26-27, 31a

Read aloud and discuss.

26 Then God said, "Let us make humankind in our image, according to our likeness; and let them have dominion over the fish of the sea, and over the birds of the air, and over the cattle, and over all the wild animals of the earth, and over every creeping thing that creeps upon the earth." 27So God created humankind in his image, in the image of God he created them; male and female created them.... 31God saw everything he had made, and indeed, it was very good.

- How can these words from Genesis help those who think poorly of themselves?
- Might some use these words to inflate their pride?
- How can we find a good balance?

Who God says we are

Read aloud.

We are unique because that is how God created us. Our very life is God's gift to us. We are the only living creatures created in God's image and that is a powerful statement of who we are. God does not create anything unworthy of praise. As Genesis says, we were created "very good."

Discuss as a group.

Consider this

"To say I am made in the image of God is to say that love is the reason for my existence, for God is love."

Thomas à Kempis

Read and discuss.

Because God knows we are fallible human beings and still accepts us, it is important that we also accept ourselves in our humanness. To be human is to be full of faults, imperfect. Perfection will come, but not in our lifetime here on earth. In 1 Corinthians 13:11-12 we read that "now we see in a mirror, dimly, but then we will see face to face. Now [we] know only in part; then [we] will know fully, even as [we] have been fully known." Our knowledge of ourselves, as it is about everything, is imperfect and complete. Yet God accepts us, is patient with us, and loves us.

Read and discuss as a group.

> **Consider this**
>
> "We ought to think very highly of ourselves, since we are God's creation, wondrously made in God's image. Moreover, we have the assurance that God loves us, knows our names, cares for our welfare, and has laid plans for us to live forever with him. To acknowledge these facts about ourselves is not to become proud and arrogant; quite to the contrary, keeping everything within this perspective would make vanity absurd."
>
> Alan Loy McGinnis, *Confidence*, page 174

Several verses in the Bible use expressions that imply we are the apple of God's eye, that is, very precious (see Psalm 17:8). If God values us so much, we can conclude that we are greatly cherished and greatly loved. Perceiving ourselves as God sees us would be a great first step. Instead, we are hard on ourselves and do not forgive our own mistakes.

Most people have casual attitudes about who another person is and what that person's performance is. We usually give others the benefit of the doubt. However, we scrutinize closely who we are and our own behavior. We tend to be our own harshest critics, our own most vocal attackers. We have to find some ways to change.

- What do you tend to criticize about yourself? Do others see that characteristic as negatively as you do?
- How do the Bible's many reassurances about God's love for us help you?

Discovery 2

Getting to know me and you

To get to know yourself and each other better, try out the three activities described here to find out a little about your personality strengths, your interests, and your skills. For each of the three activities, let everyone work individually first, then talk together.

Your personality strengths, skills, and interests

Part 1: Read through the list of personality strengths and underline the ones that describe you. Think about how you see yourself, your personality, and your outlook on life. Be as objective and realistic as possible.

Active	Empathetic	Knowledgeable
Adventurous	Encouraging	Open-minded
Affectionate	Energetic	Optimistic
Ambitious	Entertaining	Patient
Caring	Enthusiastic	Receptive
Cheerful	Friendly	Reflective
Compassionate	Helpful	Serious
Conscientious	Imaginative	Steady
Creative	Independent	Thoughtful
Dependable	Kind	Tolerant

Part 2: To identify some of your interests, on a sheet of paper list 10 things you really enjoy doing. These may include social activities, interacting with children or family members, hobbies, work, sports, amusements—whatever you wish.

Part 3: To identify a few of your skills, write down six to ten satisfying experiences or achievements. Use action verbs—organized, led, performed, made, and so forth. Achievements are things you feel you have done well, either personally or professionally; they often reveal your skills. Here are some examples: *served* as editor of our high school yearbook, *organized* a bridal shower for a friend, *reorganized* our office's layout, *built* a tree house for my children. Choose one achievement and include the where, how, what, when, and why of what you did.

Now, meet in small groups of three or four.

- For part 1, tell the others the words you underlined.
- For part 2, tell the others the interests you wrote about.
- For part 3, tell about your skills and achievements. Talk about the details you wrote down about one achievement.

Relate all of them to self-esteem. Others can make suggestions and additions as each person shares, and the recipient can tell them if they are on target.

How affirmations can help

Read aloud and discuss.

As we identify our personality strengths, our interests, and our skills, we may accept ourselves more. Another helpful technique for increasing our self-esteem is affirmations.

Affirmations are positive, supportive messages we say to ourselves. Some examples are "I will have an enjoyable day" and "I am a good problem-solver." They can replace much of our negative self-talk, such as "I know I'll mess things up." Sometimes affirming ourselves can be a challenge. While we need to be realistic with our affirmations and not say we will suddenly become genuises or win the lottery, our affirmations do need to stretch our thinking about ourselves.

- Write three to five affirmations that can help increase your self-esteem.

Discovery 3

Working on problems that hold us back

All of us have some habits or issues that bother us. This list of some common issues can help you identify one that may be affecting your self-esteem. Read them over, choose one that seems to be still giving you some trouble, and use it for the two parts that follow.

Problems and issues that inhibit self-esteem:

People-pleasing

Shame

Martyrdom

Perfectionism

Procrastination

Caretaking

Passivity

Workaholism

Need to control

Fear of rejection or abandonment

Adapted from Earnie Larson, *Stage II Recovery*, pages 19-29

Part 1: After you have chosen one, think of some time in the past when it was prominent. Sometimes a crisis such as divorce or financial difficulties make our issues even more pronounced. Our self-talk becomes negative. For instance, shame-based people tell themselves that everything is their fault. Caretakers tell themselves that they didn't do enough for someone. Perfectionists feel they must meet virtually unattainable goals or they will be failures, even in the face of evidence that others think they are great achievers.

After some time alone with the questions, meet in small groups to talk about what happened and what helped.

- As you think of your problem and your past situation, describe how it affected your self-esteem.
- What was your self-talk like?
- What were your feelings?
- What did you do to help yourself (and how did others help you) change and recover to some extent?

Part 2: Think about how that problem or issue still is with you. Identify some "stop-start" behaviors (see page 00) that may help you defuse your issue and enhance your self-esteem.

In small groups, tell each other what you plan to do. Plan to report on your progress next time you meet.

- Write two or three affirmations to say to yourself each day that are related to this issue.

- Then think of some "stop-start" actions. What will you stop doing or at least stop doing so often? What will you start doing, at least once in a while?

- To keep yourself accountable, who will you talk to after trying these for a while?

You may want to spend some time in meditation and prayer, as you think again about your gifts and your skills and the love and beauty you bring to your family and friends. When we prayerfully consider our own value, we are praising our God who has created us. By acknowledging our importance, we are recognizing that God creates only good.

Wrap-up

See page 10 in the introduction for a description of "Wrap-up."

Before you go, take time for the following:

- Group ministry task

- Review

- Personal concerns and prayer concerns

- Closing prayers

Daily walk

Bible readings

Day 1
Psalm 25:4-7

Day 2
1 John 4:7-21

Day 3
Isaiah 41:17-20

Day 4
2 Corinthians 3:1-6

Day 5
Ephesians 1:3-10

Day 6
Matthew 11:28-29

Day 7
Psalm 98:1-9

Thought for the journey

I know that I am a beautiful creation of God. God has blessed me with many gifts and talents which are important to recognize. I name them to myself and treasure them.

Prayer for the journey

Lord, help me to know myself better as I journey on my path of self-discovery. As I recognize the obstacles in my life, give me the will and strength to begin to change them. Amen.

Verse for the journey

"O Lord, you have searched me and known me.... Such knowledge is too wonderful for me; it is so high I cannot attain it" (Psalm 139:1, 6).

3 Families and Friends

Focus

The definition of self-esteem does not include being self-centered. Through all the stages of our life, healthy interpersonal relationships become possible when our self-esteem is strong.

Community building

Option

Complete this sentence: In my family, some ways we make other people feel special is _____.

What feelings are involved when family members are made to feel special and are honored?

Tell about two of your family values or practices, a traditional one and another that is somewhat unusual. These can be from your immediate family or your family of origin. Some examples are bedtime hugs, birthday parties, rules about honesty, who was in charge, roles to play, and allowances for children. Write down a brief description of them.

At the end of this activity, check to see how everyone is doing with their stop and start activities. Also, this is a good time to raise any questions regarding the small group experience or specific thoughts arising from the study material.

Opening prayer

Lord, you are with us in all of our relationships and interactions with other people. Help us to be able to show our love and affection to our families and those close to us. Amen.

Discovery 1

Our closest relationships

Read and discuss as a group.

So much of our lives is determined by the quality of our relationships. Often the most important and significant ones are those we share with family members, from both our families of origin and the families we have established. For many, there is no greater joy than to feel at home and comfortable with their families. For others, the opposite is true; their families were and may still be sources of great pain.

In some situations we may keep asking for love and affirmation from family members who can't give them to us. They may be too troubled or simply unable to give love. Going to them is like going to a dry well for water. As children we often interpret this behavior as our fault. We see ourselves as flawed or bad. When we become adults and interact with family members, the old communication and behavior patterns we experienced as children can bring these feelings of inadequacy and shame back. We feel as though we are losing the gains in self-esteem we have made. If we can't keep physical distance from those we feel harm us, we need to be clear about what the relationships will be and create some emotional distance. In these cases, we need to think of other ways to meet our needs.

Some of us may have close friends, not connected by family ties or marriage, who function as family. In an ideal world, everyone would have family members who are caring, but as long as we have people who listen, care, and are there for us, we are blessed.

A side comment: Pets as well as people can function as self-esteem builders. For instance, a dog's unconditional love and joy for its owner can do great good for that person. For children who have been abused, giving and receiving affection with an animal friend can be their first step toward recovery.

In small groups, talk about the people who nurture you and what they do or say. Also tell about what you do to nurture others and how they respond.

■ Name a couple of family members and friends. Tell how they nourish your self-esteem and enable it to grow.

We receive from others; we can also give to others. Think about spouses, children, family members, and friends whom you nurture.

■ How do your words and actions increase their self-esteem?

Self-esteem at home

During this relaxation exercise, which serves as a bridge to the next topic, the leader will help you recall memories from your childhood and youth by reading this to you.

Picture in your mind a room in your childhood home, perhaps the kitchen or living room. Think about your parent or parents, any brothers and sisters, other family members, and pets. Assume some of the people are talking. What tone of voice do the adults use? The children? [*pause*] What are your feelings—relaxed, uptight, fearful, comfortable? [*pause*] What are their actions? How are they treating each other and you? [*pause*] As you think of each one, how would you describe each person's self-esteem? [*pause*] How was your self-esteem at that time?

- Spend a few minutes jotting down your thoughts about your family of origin, their self-esteem, and yours at the time.

Meet with two or three others and talk about what you discovered from this exercise.

- Think about whether the words and behaviors you remembered were affirming or shaming.

A further look

Psalm 1:3 talks about those who follow God: "They are like trees planted by streams of water." Think about the symbolism of water—how it maintains life and makes more growth possible. In our families and with our friends, we too can be "water," that is, support systems and life-enhancers, for each other.

- What can you do to enhance the lives of those you love?
- What can you do to increase their self-esteem?

Discovery 2

Relationships through the life cycle

Read and discuss.

Thinking about the life cycle gives us some helpful perspectives on self-esteem, its origins, and its role at various times in our lives. For our purposes, family life can be divided into three time periods: childhood (infancy through age 12); adolescence through young adulthood (age 13 to about 25) and adulthood (26 to the end of life). As we look at the human life cycle briefly, we will keep in mind both our own stories and, if we have children, any connections to our role as parents.

When we are infants, our entire lives revolve around the meeting of our physical needs. We are helpless creatures who are dependent on our caregivers. When our basic needs are met, we feel secure and as a result, we feel loved and accepted and have positive feelings about ourselves. People love us and take care of us, and they respond to our needs quickly. Therefore, we assume, we must be lovable and good.

The security that we get from being loved is a process that begins at birth and continues throughout our entire childhood and adolescence. During our childhood and youth, we need support and positive reinforcement from parents and other caring adults, in order to experience a continual process of affirmation of self.

However, constructive criticism is also necessary. When parents confront their child's negative behavior, they do well to separate the behavior from the child. In other words, it is better to deal directly with the negative behavior they want to see changed than to attack the child. It is essential in any trusting relationship to be direct with our feedback, but also to offer support and care through the expected change process. The old proverb, "You get more flies with honey than with vinegar," still has validity.

Being a parent calls for wisdom, strength, and a great ability to love. Some parents may still try to change behavior with physical punishment, but many have discovered less violent ways to correct children, ones that do not damage children's self-esteem nearly as much. Timeouts work just as effectively and have the positive result of demonstrating love for the children along with a message of clear support for change.

Adolescents in particular often go through a time of low self-esteem. They see themselves in new ways and want so much to be attractive, well-liked, and successful.

Think about your own adolescence.

- In what ways was your self-esteem weak?
- How or when was it strong?
- If you have children who are adolescents, how are they doing?

Because this whole course is directed specifically to adults, let's simply acknowledge that age group and move on to a few words about life after retirement, the elder years. If we have reached our later years and still do not really value ourselves, we are likely to be bitter and fearful. On the other hand, if we know both our strengths and weaknesses and still accept ourselves, we will do just fine.

Think about some contented older people that you know.

- What are their attitudes?
- How do they relate to others?

You will probably notice that one trait such people have is a healthy attitude about themselves. Quite likely they will also have a sense of humor and the ability to laugh at the inconsistencies of life and at their own idiosyncracies. Older adults who have a high sense of self-esteem are comfortable with themselves and therefore relate well with others.

A further look

Romans 8:16 says "we are children of God."

- What does this say about our value?
- If we are secure in the knowledge that we are God's children, how might we be able to react when others reject us?

Discovery 3

John 15:9-12

Read and discuss.

⁹As the Father has loved me, so I have loved you; abide in my love. ¹⁰If you keep my commandments, you will abide in my love, just as I have kept my Father's commandments and abide in his love. ¹¹I have said these things to you so that my joy may be in you, and that your joy may be complete. ¹²This is my commandment, that you love one another as I have loved you.

Loving God and others

As we hear Jesus' words about loving others, we may wonder how we can love ourselves, love others, and love God. How can we do all three? Perhaps those last two words offer us a clue: love God.

A strong spiritual foundation, based on trust in the loving God who created us, gives us the courage to reach out to others and still nurture and love ourselves. God will help us meet our own needs and also meet others' needs. In our spiritual life, we have access to many "building blocks" that can help us. They include reading the Bible and other books, prayer, writing in a journal, going on retreat, talking to friends who are spiritually aware, ministering to others, and participating in the activities and services of a church or spiritual community.

- ■ Which of those building blocks do you rely on?
- ■ Which are relatively new to you but ones you would like to try?

When we feel confused and unsure about which direction to go, we need to turn to God for help. God promises to guide us continually (see Isaiah 58:11) and gives us inner strength and faith to keep going. We can be sure we will eventually be led to the resources we need.

- ■ What connections do you see between your faith and self-esteem?
- ■ Recall a time when you faced a major crisis. Think about your faith and your level of self-esteem. What roles did they play in the outcome?

Read aloud and discuss.

Consider this

Psalm 90:1-6 puts the human journey into a different perspective. Even when we feel small compared to the grandeur of creation, God knows us by name, cares for us, and loves us.

- How do you feel when you consider your life as part of the broader fabric of creation?

As part of our spiritual growth, we need to keep working on self-esteem issues. You can look at the stop and start behaviors you already have tried, and continue them or find new ones. You can spend time in prayer and then work on small positive changes. Be realistic about them. It's a good idea to talk to a trusted friend, relative, or member of this group and ask that person to give you some feedback about your changes and how you are doing.

A further look

Explore and relate.

Romans 12:3 tells us we should not think of ourselves more highly than we ought to think. Galatians 6:2-5 tells us to be willing to bear one another's burdens and to watch where we place our pride. How do humility and bearing others' burdens fit with high self-esteem?

- Where is the balance between thinking well of ourselves and meeting the needs of others?

Wrap-up

Before you go, take time for the following:

- Group ministry task

- Review

- Personal concerns and prayer concerns

- Closing prayers

Daily walk

Bible readings

Day 1
Psalm 96:1-9

Day 2
Ephesians 3:14-21

Day 3
2 Peter 3:8-13

Day 4
John 15:1-11

Day 5
Philippians 4:4-11

Day 6
Galatians 3:25-29

Day 7
Ecclesiastes 3:1-8

Thought for the journey

Because healthy and loving relationships give great meaning to our lives, we continue to explore ways to love ourselves, others, and God.

Prayer for the journey

Dear God, be with me as I continue my journey of self-discovery and growth. I know that you created me, love me, and guide me, so with your help, I am able to change and grow. Amen.

Verse for the journey

"Do to others as you would have them do to you" (Luke 6:31).

4 The Wider World of Relationships

Focus

Our friendships and social contacts fill many needs in our lives. As we build healthy relationships, our self-esteem grows.

Community building

Meet in small groups and take turns giving responses.

Talk about ideas generated by the study and ideas from the daily walk. Also check with each other to see how you are doing with stop and start activities.

We will be looking at relationships that develop in the wider world of our jobs and social activities. Think of one setting, perhaps your job, school, church, or where you volunteer, and complete these two thought-starters.

- Here's how I would describe my self-esteem when I am doing work or activities I enjoy:

- Here's how I would describe my self-esteem when I am doing work or activities I don't enjoy very much:

Option

Try this word association game. Each participant is to say three words that come to mind when a key word is said.

The first key word is *work*. If time allows, also try *volunteer, conflict,* and *respect*.

Opening prayer

Dear Lord, work with us as we explore our work and social relationships. Help us to build healthy attitudes and the skills we need for being good friends and coworkers. Amen.

Discovery 1

Romans 12:9-16, 21

Read aloud and discuss.

⁹Let love be genuine; hate what is evil, hold fast to what is good; ¹⁰love one another with mutual affection; outdo one another in showing honor. ¹¹Do not lag in zeal, be ardent in spirit, serve the Lord. ¹²Rejoice in hope, be patient in suffering, persevere in prayer. ¹³Contribute to the needs of the saints; extend hospitality to strangers. ¹⁴Bless those who persecute you; bless and do not curse them. ¹⁵Rejoice with those who rejoice, weep with those who weep. ¹⁶Live in harmony with one another; do not be haughty, but associate with the lowly; do not claim to be wiser than you are.... ²¹Do not be overcome by evil, but overcome evil with good.

This beautiful passage describes a family of actions that, if practiced by a majority of us, would change the world. Given our flawed ability to be all that we are meant to be, we can nevertheless use these words as a guide for our relationships with others.

Explore and relate.

- ■ Note the many imperatives that tell us what to do. Underline about ten of the words of command that speak clearly to you.

- ■ Then choose one verse and say how you try to live it in your daily life.

Our wider friendships

Read and discuss.

How much we need other people! If we take a few minutes to look back on our lives, we see how important other people were to us—our families especially, but also our friends. We were created to be social beings, to love and be loved.

Other people give us perspectives our narrow worlds would not provide. They help us see more around us, but they also help us see more about ourselves. John Bradshaw quotes a notice from a drug rehabilitation agency: "We are here because there is no escape finally from ourselves. Until a person confronts himself in the eyes and hearts of others, he is running. Where else but in our common ground can we find such a mirror... together we can take root and grow... not as the giant of our dreams or the dwarf of our fears, but as a man/woman... part of a whole with a share in its purpose" (John Bradshaw, *Creating Love*, page 279).

With others, we find out more clearly who we are. With others, we see our value. With others, we get our dreams and fears into a more balanced perspective. With others, we learn to love and be loved.

- Why is self-esteem so closely connected to our interactions with other people? Doesn't the word self in self-esteem imply that we could make real accomplishments working on it in isolation?
- How have the members of this group helped you value yourself and see yourself more clearly?

Discovery 2

The workplace and other social settings

The problems and possibilities that our self-esteem experiences with family and close friends are very similar to those it encounters in our work and with our secondary personal contacts. For instance, if we struggle with shame in our families, feelings of shame might also follow us to work. To continue in our growth, we need to be aware of what happens to our self-esteem as we interact with people in our jobs, church, school, and many other social settings.

People feel good about their jobs and other activities when they feel they are doing important work. It doesn't matter if they are assembling quality cars or being proficient at teaching. The important fact is that they want to be proud of what they do. "In all that you do, do it well" is a motto that is shared by most people with high self-esteem. That is true if you are self-employed and working in the home, or part of the production line in a giant corporation.

Read and discuss.

Consider this

Read 2 Timothy 2:15. We are to do our best to present ourselves to God as workers who have no need to feel ashamed. In other words, we are to do the best we can and live up to our values in the workplace.

- What are some of the ways our faith can show in our work?
- What are some of the ways high self-esteem helps us in our work?

Read aloud and discuss.

But some people make their work into an idol. The entire focus of their lives is being with "the company" or having the prestige that goes with their job. People who work out of their home or are self-employed can make the same mistake. Workaholism or any other type of addiction harms self-esteem.

Some may find themselves in a position where their own spiritual values and commitments are in a collision course with their work expectations. A graduate student struggled when she was asked by her adviser to present only part of their research; he wanted to cover up some of the findings. A man in his fifties did not want to substitute the inferior materials for the high-quality ones that were specified, but he was told to do it or his job would be in jeopardy. The issues are complex and difficult, and can create great stress for people with high values.

- While respecting anonymity, talk about a situation you know that involves questionable compromises at work.

Companies, schools, churches, clubs, and other social organizations are like extended families. The dynamics that operate in family systems are also at work in social situations. The simple fact of life is that when we go to work, school, church, or organizations, we take our personality and the values we hold "near and dear" with us to the job or social setting.

In a family system, different people take on specific roles. Some hold positions of power and some are followers. Others become caretakers, placators, or negotiators. A social situation, like a family, can become dysfunctional if people can't change their roles.

Discuss as a group.

Consider this

Psalm 33:15 tells us that God fashions our hearts and observes all our deeds. God is aware of the work we do in our lives. When the work of our hands, our hearts, and our minds does not match our values, we experience conflict and our self-esteem suffers.

- **What role do your faith and the values deriving from it play in your job, schoolwork, or volunteer commitments?**

Sometimes our self-esteem suffers when we say nothing about unfair behaviors, letting them continue in our job or volunteer environment. Perhaps some discrimination is going on, and women or people of color are not being treated fairly. We may not be comfortable with disagreement and say, "It's none of my business." Yet, buried in our minds lie the thoughts, "I should have done something when I saw this happening," or "If only I had intervened, this wouldn't have happened."

Our inaction can affect our self-esteem. We feel guilty if we think we "should" have done something or "if only" we had taken action. We need to watch out when "if only" and "should" come together! When we use those words regularly, we will not feel good about ourselves. How much better to take some action. We probably don't need to do it all alone; others are likely to have seen what we have seen.

- While respecting anonymity, tell about a situation where you needed to speak up in order to prevent unfair treatment.

A further look

Read and discuss.

Read Genesis 25:29-34. This story about Esau selling his birthright to his conniving brother Jacob has implications for us in regard to honesty and compromise in the workplace.

- How might we be tempted to compromise our standards and our spiritual values when some aspects of our work are in conflict with them?
- What happens to our self-esteem if we do?

Discovery 3

Matthew 5:14-16

Read aloud and discuss.

14"You are the light of the world. A city built on a hill cannot be hid. 15No one after lighting a lamp puts it under the bushel basket, but on the lampstand, and it gives light to all in the house. 16In the same way, let your light shine before others, so that they may see your good works, and give glory to your Father in heaven."

Here we have another passage that gives our self-esteem a boost. We are to be light! Jesus has faith that we can shine, that we can do things that are good, and that those works will glorify God. Being so valued, we dare to move beyond ourselves and let our goodness shine.

Called to be lights

Read and discuss as a group.

In New York, a woman who had broken up with her boyfriend some months ago called her counselor. "But I have so much love to give!" she cried. The counselor knew the woman was implying that she wanted another boyfriend, but on another level, the counselor thought of all the need in New York and how many people the woman could find who would appreciate some love and kindness.

Alan Loy McGinnis, in his book *Confidence*, says that a key for people wanting to enhance their self-esteem is to build a network of loving, accepting relationships. "Progress comes when they are able to relax, stop begging for love, and begin loving. They look for someone for whom they can do a favor, someone whose shoulder they can put an arm around, and perhaps even begin to love. When we are 'networking' merely for what we can get out of it, it usually backfires. But when we start finding others who need love and take the initiative in giving it to them, love seems to begin flowing back to us" (Alan Loy McGinnis, *Confidence*, page 160).

Discuss as a group.

Consider this

Matthew 25:34-40 tells that Jesus said to those who had fed the hungry and ministered to people who were in need, "Just as you did it to one of the least of these who are members of my family, you did it to me." They were surprised to hear Jesus' words. People who are full of love, having been loved, may hardly even realize the good they are doing. It is the work of God. By ourselves we would not be able to do much, but when God's power, love, and wisdom work through us, our lights can shine brightly.

- How has this been true in your life?
- How has this been true in the lives of people you know?

Read aloud.

McGinnis says we can have great self-esteem without turning it into pride as long as we are always looking for places to serve and to love. He tells of author Evelyn Underhill who sought advice from her mentor. He suggested, among other things, that she leave her books and spend two afternoons a week among poor persons in the slums of London (Alan Loy McGinnis, *Confidence*, page 175-176). We all need to find ways to let our light shine, and one thing we can do is to work among those who suffer and who need our love.

God guides us to places where we feel wonderful to be there. God knows us, our personalities, interests, skills, and ability. Some might want to work with animals or to preserve the environment. Many others might findways to work with people, perhaps through their churches. We do have gifts to share. God calls us to shine and give others light. Our light may not seem very large, but we do not know how God will multiply its benefits. We might agree with Eleanor Roosevelt who said she would rather light one candle than curse the darkness.

- To what place has God guided you where you feel wonderful?
- What one candle would you like to light rather than curse the darkness?

A further look

Explore and relate.

Read James 2:14-17. We may claim to have great faith and to be very loving, but our actions show whether we are telling the truth.

- When we do not live by what we say, what might happen to our self-esteem?

Wrap-up

Before you go, take time for the following:

- Group ministry task

- Review

- Personal concerns and prayer concerns

- Closing prayers

Daily walk

Bible readings

Day 1
Psalm 121:1-8

Day 2
Galatians 6:1-6

Day 3
Isaiah 55:6-13

Day 4
Ephesians 4:25-32

Day 5
Luke 6:27-36

Day 6
1 Timothy 6:11-16

Day 7
Hebrews 13:1-6

Prayer for the journey

My work and social contacts give me opportunities to keep growing and to use my gifts so that both others and myself will be blessed.

Thought for the journey

God, in all of my social interactions, help me to be all that you want me to be. Thank you for the gift of other people. They give so much to me; help me to be able to give to them. Amen.

Verse for the journey

"Above all, maintain constant love for one another, for love covers a multitude of sins" (1 Peter 4:8).

5 The Matter of Appearance

Focus

Our self-image, the way we see and define ourselves, includes what we think about our physical appearance. Being able to accept how we look increases our self-esteem.

Community building

A volunteer may distribute the slips of paper to the participants as they enter the room.

Talk with other participants to see how you are coming on stop and start activities, and if there are any questions or concerns.

The leader has written the name of a famous person who has public appeal on the piece of paper you received as you entered the room. Try to pantomime the identity of the person. If the others cannot guess, add brief word clues.

When other group members guess the name of the person you were acting out, sign your initials on the back of the others' papers.

When everyone has finished, see how many of you were able to identify those famous people.

- What traits were easily identifiable and what traits were more difficult?
- Did physical appearances or mannerisms make a contribution?

Option

Think of a person who has been in the media and complete the sentence, "_____(name) is physically beautiful or handsome because _____." Talk with each other briefly about what you wrote. Then talk about what those persons might experience if something happened to change or disfigure their bodies.

Opening prayer

As we live each day, dear God, help us to keep everything in perspective. We thank you for our bodies, but help us to remember that we are much more than our bodies. Amen.

Discovery 1

Psalm 8:3-9

Read and discuss as a group.

³ **When I look at your heavens, the work of your fingers,**
  the moon and the stars that you have established;
⁴ **what are human beings that you are mindful of them,**
  mortals that you care for them?
⁵ **Yet you have made them a little lower than God,**
  and crowned them with glory and honor.
⁶ **You have given them dominion over the works of your hands;**
  you have put all things under their feet,
⁷ **all sheep and oxen,**
  and also the beasts of the field,
⁸ **the birds of the air, and the fish of the sea,**
  whatever passes along the paths of the sea.
⁹ **O Lord, our Sovereign,**
  how majestic is your name in all the earth!

God gave us bodies

This hymn of praise celebrates God's glory and the dignity of the human beings God created. When we are tempted to put ourselves down, we need to remember who created us and what a high place we were given in creation. In some translations, verse 5 reads, "Yet you have made them a little lower than the angels." We are right up there! God has given us great honor.

This psalm tells us that we are meant to hold a high place, but it also helps us keep some healthy humility. We are not God. We are a little lower than God and the angels. Our task is to care for creation.

- After hearing or reading news reports about the messes human beings get into, have you ever felt like asking God questions similar to the one in verse 4, "Why do you even bother yourself with us, God?"

- When have you felt like asking questions like that?

- If you had been an adviser to God at creation, would you have recommended that human beings have a different kind of body?

- What would that new human body be like—just as physical as it is now, or less physical?

Read aloud.

We tend to present ourselves to the world according to how we think we look. We may even think that the way we look determines how much we can achieve in the world and who will like us or care to associate with us. The part of our self-image that is connected to our appearance can be a boost or a burden to other areas of our self-esteem. A man who just received a promotion might discount it, saying he knew he was chosen for his good looks. A woman awarded a commendation at work might say, "Yes, they say I did fine, but I'm so homely I don't think I'll go to the awards banquet."

- ■ Take a few minutes to think about how some of your negative self-talk about your appearance began. If you can, recall two kinds of memories from your childhood and your youth:

    a. Words said to you by *others* that negatively affected what you thought about your appearance.

    b. Words, evaluations, and judgments you yourself made about your appearance.

Meet with two or three others to discuss your memories and how you were able to let them go.

- ■ After identifying some negative memories, ask yourself if any of them still bother you.

- ■ Also think about how you were able to let disparaging comments go, and to get on with your life.

Read and discuss as a group.

People usually do not want to be too different from others. Their ideal image of themselves is to be accepted by the group. Each of us knows what we want to be like and how we want to appear to other people. Unfortunately, some do not feel accepted because they are members of a different race from the majority. Sometimes women feel excluded, as do other groups who are not completely accepted.

Sometimes we recite a list of our body's unattractive qualities—the thick thighs we inherited from Grandma, our large nose, our thin hair. We think we have little beauty to offer. In actuality, God made us all beautiful and gifted. We may notice, however, that our beauty and gifts vary quite a bit.

If we asked all the people we met for one week how they would like to be physically different, we might be surprised at the variety of answers. Among them would probably be height, weight, shape of body, proportions, strength, shape or position of eyes, hair or lack of it, coloring, and features they didn't like. Often the very characteristic that one person wants to change appears attractive to another.

John Bradshaw, in his book *Creating Love*, uses charts to show how we tend to think in extremes. Regarding our physical appearance, the people on one end of the scale spend a great deal of time and money on packaging themselves (exaggerated concern for hair, skin, clothes, and so on). The people on the other end think they are ugly anyway so they don't bother to do anything and end up looking sloppy. (See John Bradshaw, *Creating Love*, page 276.)

- How would you describe the people at the two extremes?
- What would you expect their self-esteem to be like?
- What would be a good middle ground for taking care of our physical appearance?
- How would that choice relate to self-esteem?

A further look

Read and discuss.

Read Psalm 139:13-18. The psalmist says we are "fearfully and wonderfully made" and that God has known us from our mother's womb.

- What does this tell us about the value of our physical selves?
- If God created us, knows us, and cares for us, how can we discount our value?

Discovery 2

Matthew 6:19-21

Read and discuss.

¹⁹"Do not store up for yourselves treasures on earth, where moth and rust consume and where thieves break in and steal; ²⁰but store up for yourselves treasures in heaven, where neither moth nor rust consumes and where thieves do not break in and steal. ²¹For where your treasure is, there your heart will be also."

When our appearance changes

An overemphasis on physical attractiveness is similar to the treasures mentioned in this passage. They are not lasting. If looking young and beautiful is vitally important to us, our happiness is in jeopardy if our body is ever damaged or when it gets old.

When a person's appearance suddenly changes from an accident or surgery, his or her self-image is likely to suffer. That person needs to rethink life and its meaning, and might very well need professional help to work things through.

- Read the three examples given below. What might happen to the self-esteem of these people? Who or what could help them?

    a. A man who has been popular and active has an accident that leaves him disfigured and disabled.

    b. An executive whose identity is connected to her work has a sudden heart attack and is told to put her job on hold.

    c. A young person using an electric saw damages his or her hand so severely that it will always be misshapen.

Add examples from your own life, thinking about the overall impact of what happened and how it changed how you felt about yourself.

Consider this

In John 13:34, Jesus said, "Love one another as I have loved you." We know Jesus loves us. Those words directly tell us our worth. For if our Savior Jesus Christ finds us worthy of his love, then we are worth more than we can ever imagine. Measure your worth through the eyes of Christ and you will have a true measure.

Read and discuss.

Given the fragility of the human body, nearly everyone will have to face changes in appearance. Unless we die young, we will age, and as we do so we lose some of our beauty. Our skin wrinkles and dries to some extent, our hair is likely to turn gray or fall out, and our body will lose some of its youthful shape and flexibility.

Other things matter more than physical beauty, yet we often go through a time of grieving and adjustment when our appearance changes, especially if the changes are obvious and severe.

In addition to aging, a number of other conditions can cause change in appearance. Among them are weight gain or loss and various diseases and disabilities, such as multiple sclerosis, that affect mobility.

- Think of events from your own life when your appearance changed. What was the overall impact of what happened and how did it change how you felt about yourself?

- How can you help others who have been hurt, lost their hair during cancer treatments, or are getting old? What can you say and do to help them?

A further look

Read aloud and discuss.

In 2 Corinthians 12:7-10 Paul wrote about the calamities that had befallen him, including a "thorn in the flesh" that God did not choose to remove. He concluded, "Therefore I am content with weaknesses, insults, hardships, persecutions, and calamities for the sake of Christ; for whenever I am weak, then I am strong."

- In what ways can illnesses and other physical problems sometimes contribute to our strength?

- What is the role of our faith during troubled times?

Discovery 3

Where our culture leads us

Read and discuss as a group.

Much of our culture is projected through television ads. The advertisers appeal to our senses on behalf of every conceivable kind of product. Usually, handsome men and beautiful women deliver these advertisements. This implies that if we buy the product, we too will become as attractive as the models who appeal to our hearts and wallets. We are inundated with pictures of what life could be like if only we bought and did what the media suggests.

Children are particularly vulnerable to the media. Many children become unhappy when their parents don't purchase some object advertised during the cartoon shows. But what is being sold is really a concept—if you want to be accepted by others, you must have this toy, doll, or article of clothing. If you are an adult, you are similarly pressured to buy the new model car or the fashionable brand of beer. Without the advertised product, you will not belong to the "in" crowd.

Many well-known people, past and present, would be judged as failures if we used our culture's ideals of physical beauty. Napoleon Bonaparte was short. Luciano Pavarotti is overweight. Jimmy Durante's nose was large. Golda Meir knew she was not a beauty.

Golda Meir felt inferior when she was young because she knew beauty was something she would never have. At last she came to the point when "being called pretty no longer had any importance." Instead, she set out to find what she wanted to do in life, and she did it (Alan Loy McGinnis, *Confidence*, page 32).

Part of accepting the way our bodies look, our race, our gender, and all our physical characteristics goes back to knowing what really matters. People on their deathbeds rarely talk about their appearance, their possessions, or other remembrances of physical concerns. Instead, they talk about thankfulness for the people whom they loved and who loved them. We are back to the beginning once more. The heart of the matter is loving ourselves, loving others, and loving God.

Meet in small groups to discuss the qualities of the people you named.

- Think of someone you know personally who would not be considered beautiful by many people, but who is someone you admire.
- What qualities other than physical beauty does this person have?
- How much does physical beauty matter in the long run?

A further look

Read and discuss.

In the passage from Proverbs that describes a virtuous woman, we read "Charm is deceitful, and beauty is vain, but a woman who fears the LORD is to be praised" (Proverbs 31:30). This implies that beauty and charm are fickle. They can be gone in the twinkling of an eye, but the inner qualities such as faith and reverence, which is what "fear" means here, count much more.

- Do you know a woman like this?
- How about a man?
- Do you think our culture believes that other things can count more than beauty?

Wrap-up

Before you go, take time for the following:

- Group ministry task

- Review

- Personal concerns and prayer concerns

- Closing prayers

Daily walk

Bible readings

Day 1
1 Samuel 16:6-13

Day 2
Psalm 103:1-5, 15-18

Day 3
Matthew 20:29-34

Day 4
Psalm 51:10-12, 15-17

Day 5
2 Corinthians 12:7-10

Day 6
Galatians 6:7-10

Day 7
Revelation 21:1-4

Thought for the journey

Having a physical body gives us many opportunities to keep learning what life is all about. When I accept who I am, I can take care of my physical concerns but keep them balanced with everything else that is important to me.

Prayer for the journey

Lord, open our eyes so that we are able to see our true worth. Guide us in our journey of self-acceptance, including acceptance of our bodies as unique and lovable. Amen.

Verse for the journey

"Do you not know that you are God's temple and that God's Spirit dwells in you?" (1 Corinthians 3:16).

6 Confidently on Our Way

Focus

A healthy sense of self-esteem helps us live each day to the fullest. As we look to the future, we feel reassured by what we have learned about loving ourselves, loving others, and loving God.

Community building

Option

Using paper and markers, draw "before and after" pictures or symbols. The first one should show how you felt about yourself before this group began; the second should show how you are feeling now.

In the space below, write about these two topics:

- What has happened with your self-esteem during this small group?
- What else do you feel you gained from the sessions?

Talk together with a partner or in small groups.

Opening prayer

Lord, you are with us through everything that happens in our lives. We thank you for all the blessings in the past and ask that you be with us now as we look to the future. Amen.

Discovery 1

It's about love

Read and discuss.

Our starting point for this small group experience was to focus on self-esteem, but as we moved along, we have discovered that a strong second theme is love. We know that it is from loving and being loved that self-esteem best emerges, and ultimately it is God's love that is the foundation of both.

Colossians 3:12-14, 17

¹²"As God's chosen ones, holy and beloved, clothe yourselves with compassion, kindness, humility, meekness, and patience. ¹³Bear with one another and, if anyone has a complaint against another, forgive each other; just as the Lord has forgiven you, so you also must forgive. ¹⁴Above all, clothe yourselves with love, which binds everything together in perfect harmony.... ¹⁷And whatever you do, in word or deed, do everything in the name of the Lord Jesus, giving thanks to God the Father through him."

- What role does forgiveness play in our relationships with ourselves, others, and God?
- What does forgiveness have to do with self-esteem?
- Have you had any experiences of "love binding everything together in perfect harmony"? Because perfection is rare in this life, recall a time when love created "nearly perfect" harmony for you or someone you know.

Discuss as a group.

Consider this

"It is the love of God that provides the foundation of our identities, and because we are then given such a peaceful center—such a point of reference that keep us mentally sound—we are able to turn and give ourselves to others. The paradox is that such giving of ourselves to our neighbors does not threaten our self-image, but rather reinforces it. The amazing thing about love, Rollo May [a well-known writer on love, intimacy, and self-esteem] says, is that it is the best way to get to know ourselves. Self-confidence, like happiness, is slippery when we set out to grab it for its own sake. Usually it comes rather as a by-product. We lose ourselves in service, and suddenly one day we awake to realize that we are confident and happy."

Alan Loy McGinnis, *Confidence*, page 178

> **Consider this**
>
> "We are to love ourselves as God loves us: God is not overly impressed with us—he knows our flaws. But we are God's children, and God is benevolently interested in our welfare. So if we are to call it 'self-love,' we must see it as this relaxed appreciation and healthy regard for the beloved."
>
> Alan Loy McGinnis, Confidence, page 179
>
> ◼ Talk about the paradox mentioned in the first quote by McGinnis and his description of self-love in the second.
>
> ◼ Do you agree or disagree with what he says?

A further look

Read aloud and discuss.

Read Matthew 5:43-44. We are called to love our enemies. We might be surprised to see who Carl Jung included as enemies in the quotation that follows.

"There is no doubt in my mind that a deep understanding of and a serious effort to achieve true love of self is the beginning of all human growth and happiness.... [We would like to quote] Carl Jung, from his book, *Modern Man in Search of a Soul:* 'the acceptance of self is the essence of the moral problem and the epitome of a whole outlook upon life. That I feed the hungry, that I forgive an insult, that I love my enemy in the name of Christ—all these are undoubtedly great virtues. What I do unto the least of my brethren, that I do unto Christ. But what if I should discover that the least amongst them all, the poorest of the beggars, the most impudent of all the offenders, the very enemy himself—that these are within me, and I that I myself stand in need of the alms of my own kindness—that I myself am the enemy who must be loved—what then?'"

John Powell, The Secret of Staying in Love, page 19

◼ In what ways do we show our frequent dislike of ourselves?

◼ How do we make enemies of ourselves?

◼ What are the implications of the quote from Carl Jung about forgiveness? About self-love?

Discovery 2

The need for balance

Read aloud and discuss as a group.

Healthy self-esteem is ultimately linked to balance. In terms of how we care for our bodies, as we saw in Session 5, we can do too much or too little. In terms of time, if we work or play or watch TV for too much time, not enough time is left for other things in our lives.

When our lives are out of balance, we are harder on ourselves and our self-esteem suffers. The following exercise will help us think about how we balance the various aspects of our lives. We need to keep in mind the spiritual, emotional, mental, physical, occupational, financial, and social dimensions of life, among others. From your responses, you may see some directions you would like to move in your life. These can be useful for the next activity, goal setting.

Answer **Y** (yes), **U** (unsure), or **N** (no) to these items.

_____ a. I take time for reading the Bible and devotional books and for prayer.

_____ b. I go to church regularly.

_____ c. I get adequate exercise each week.

_____ d. I am able to maintain a weight that is appropriate for my height and body build.

_____ e. I eat healthy foods in moderate portions.

_____ f. I am able to handle my mortgage or rent payments and basic living expenses fairly well.

_____ g. I feel good about the amount of money I am able to give to my church and other good causes.

_____ h. I spend enough time with my loved ones.

_____ i. I regularly keep in touch (phone, letters, in person) with several close friends.

_____ j. I seldom feel overly anxious.

_____ k. I have someone I can talk to openly about my feelings and concerns.

_____ l. I keep my mind alert by reading, going to classes, hearing speakers, or by conversing with informed friends.

_____ m. I leave my work problems at work and relax when I am home.

_____ n. I find ways to help to others on my own or through volunteer opportunities.

_____ o. I have fun or do something playful and relaxing every week.

Adapted from *'Tis a Gift to Be Simple*, by Barbara DeGrote-Sorensen and David Allen Sorensen, pages 37-41

Meet with two or three others to discuss your answers.

- Talk briefly about which items you marked *Y*.
- Look at those you marked *U* and *N*. These are good candidates for future goals.
- Ask yourselves what would happen to your self-esteem if you could change your answer on some of the items to *yes*.

Read and discuss.

This second exercise asks you to think about how to balance some emphases that have been mentioned in this course. Each topic displays a continuum between two extremes. Briefly think about the dangers of going to either extreme. Then write down a few words that describe a healthy balance for each topic.

Taking care of myself	Taking care of others
Thinking I am 100% wonderful	Thinking I am a total loser
Thinking nothing is my fault	Thinking everything is my fault
Being super-responsible	Being super-irresponsible
How my life turns out depends on God	How my life turns out depends on me

- After completing the exercise, meet with a partner to discuss healthy balances for the five items.

Discovery 3

Read aloud and discuss.

Goals and dreams

The members of Alcoholics Anonymous are encouraged to live AA's Twelve Steps on a daily basis. Steps 4 and 5 have the members take a self-inventory and share it with another human being. What happens in these two steps is that a person begins a new period in his or her journey into self-knowledge.

By looking at ourselves through new eyes, we can know ourselves more fully and come to terms with who we are. We have looked at ourselves a number of times in this small group. Self-inventories need to include the positive too, not just the negative. We may think that if we acknowledge our beautiful traits and our gifts, we are being vain. This is not true. We need to give ourselves permission to love what is good in ourselves. This positive reinforcement increases our self-esteem. Self-fulfilling prophecies are usually thought of as negative, but they can work in positive directions, too. When we believe that we can succeed, our chances of success are much higher.

- What have you learned about yourself from the various activities in this small group? Include both negatives and positives.
- If you are willing, share some of your insights with a partner.

An invitation to change

Discuss as a group.

Here is something you might like to try. It has been said that it takes 21 days to change a habit. Think of something you would like to change about yourself that is related to your self-esteem, perhaps being more patient with people. Write an affirmation or two that will encourage you to do it. Every morning and evening for the next three weeks, stand in front of a mirror (full length is best) and look yourself directly in the eye. Tell yourself your positive messages as if you were talking to a cherished friend. Each day give the same, consistent message to yourself. Be firm and positive in your approach.

As the days go by, practice your new attitude and related behaviors in all of your interactions with other people. Do not let yourself slip into your old thinking patterns or behaviors. Remember, this is a time to allow yourself to believe you are changing. At the end of the three-week period, notice the outcome. Ask yourself what you learned about yourself during that time and how you feel now.

Setting some goals

Life is a series of events that when taken as single entities do not make much sense. Yet, when we look at the overall pattern, we can see some meaning. As you recall your past experiences, identify some that fit into a pattern. You can set some goals to lead to positive changes when you can identify patterns of behavior.

As we have discovered, there really are many different ways to raise self-esteem, but they all take time and effort. This implies that we need to be intentional about goal setting.

We "can do" many things for ourselves, and we "can change" some things. The important realization is that the only changes we can make are those that involve ourselves. We cannot make other people change—something we need to keep in mind. But if we see a need in ourselves, we can change our attitudes, our beliefs, our values, and our actions.

However, as we set goals, we need to remember that there are some things we cannot change about ourselves. We cannot make some physical illness or disability disappear. We cannot change many of our physical characteristics. We cannot rewrite our past. We need to be realistic about our changes.

If you set some goals several weeks ago when this small group met for the first time, look them over (see page 73). You may have met them, but you may want to expand on them or choose some new ones.

On a sheet of paper, write three goals. Choose one of them and write down some hindering and helping factors. If you wish, share what you have written with a partner.

- ■ Write down three goals that you are most committed to, are most excited about, and are willing to work toward.

- ■ Do a "force field analysis." That is, think about and write down what might prevent you from reaching your goals and what will help you meet them. Identify factors that might hinder you (lack of time, no support group) and helping factors (enough time, friends support you).

- ■ If you can eliminate some negatives and build on your positives, you will make progress. Make a contract with yourself to find the support and resources you need to meet your goals.

> **Consider this**
>
> Psalm 121 has beautiful words of comfort for the times we feel insecure and in need of reassurance.
>
> - As you read this passage, reflect on your worries and on the tasks you see ahead of you.
>
> - What do we learn here about God's presence and support for us in our daily lives?

An invitation to accept yourself

Read and discuss.

Finally, you are invited to come to the realization that you are a very special person with very special talents. You are "one of a kind." As you move forward and learn more about yourself, practice acceptance of your own individuality. You have gifts to share with other people and it is important that you come to understand and value what they are. Be honest and bold with your assessment of yourself. Then, move out into the world around you, knowing you are loved and willing to love others.

A further look

Read and discuss as a group.

Jesus told three parables regarding the kingdom of God in Matthew 13:44-48, mentioning a treasure in a field, a pearl, and a net full of fish. Each of these parables refers to an inner motivation that spurred people into action when they found something of great worth. So it is when we realize how much God loves us and how we can live that love in our lives. We know we have found something of great worth, probably beyond our human minds' abilities to understand.

Wrap-up

Before you go, take time for the following:

- **Group ministry task**

- **Review**

- **Personal concerns and prayer concerns**

- **Closing prayers**

Daily walk

Bible readings

Day 1
Psalm 136:1-3, 23-26

Day 2
Philippians 3:12-16

Day 3
Isaiah 51:12-13, 16

Day 4
James 1:17-18

Day 5
Psalm 34:15-18

Day 6
John 10:1-10

Day 7
Galatians 5:22-25

Prayer for the journey

I have lived with myself all the days of my life, but I keep learning about myself and seeing new ways to grow and to reach out to others.

Thought for the journey

Lord, you love me and created me to love and be loved. Thank you for helping me realize how important my contributions can be to other people and to you. Amen.

Verse for the journey

"Now may our Lord Jesus Christ himself and God our Father, who loved us and through grace gave us eternal comfort and good hope, comfort your hearts and strengthen them in every good work and word" (2 Thessalonians 2:16-17).

Facilitator helps

The experiences group members have as they use the material in this course could change their lives. They will learn about themselves, the others in the group, basic principles and strategies related to self-esteem, and some basic teachings of the Christian faith. As they learn and participate, they will feel good about themselves and their self-esteem will become stronger. The participants will go through a whole range of feelings, from sadness over past mistakes and problems to real joy.

Is this a therapy group?

All these good things will happen, but even though a significant amount of healing may take place, this group is not a therapy group. At the first session, you will need to point out the difference between therapy groups and support and recovery groups. Generally speaking, therapy groups have the purpose of assisting people to work through deeper issues and problems in their lives, including addictions, depression, unhealed traumas, and mental illnesses. Support and recovery groups emphasize education and enrichment, although there is the hope that considerable growth and recovery will also take place.

As the participants talk about the roots of their self-esteem, they may bring up serious issues that may have deeply affected them, such as alcohol or drug-related concerns, infidelity, incest, and domestic violence issues. Any one of these areas has the potential to be more than a support and recovery group can handle. Be sure to recommend professional services to those with complex and deep-seated problems.

Is therapy needed?

Here are some indications that some individuals may need therapy:

- The person's problems are severe and intense, perhaps related to family of origin, marriage, children, or job.
- The person has a chronic problem that is not under control, such as alcoholism or drug use.
- The person refuses the help of others in the group.
- The person is severely depressed.

As part of the preparation process, it is helpful for the facilitator and the pastor or priest to meet ahead of time. During this meeting, a system can be arranged to give the facilitator information about referral sources for group members who need additional assistance.

What about depression?

It is worth a moment to take a look at depression. Depression is a disease that affects about 12.5 percent of the population at any given time. Approximately 80 percent of these people go untreated. In the United States about 32 million people are affected by the disease, meaning that 25.6 million (80 percent of that number) have not received treatment. Depression is a serious illness which has enormous impact on self-esteem. When people are depressed, their whole life is affected.

Chronic symptoms of depression are apathy, low self-esteem, low energy, poor appetite, abnormal sleeping patterns (too much, too little), early morning awakening, weight gain or loss, and feeling hopeless and helpless. People who exhibit these symptoms need immediate referral to a health professional.

If you are aware that some individuals are threatening suicide or are having suicidal thoughts, they too need to be seen immediately by a professional. Those are life-threatening situations which demand immediate response.

What about abuse?

If sexual abuse survivors bring up traumatic issues from their past, it is important to allow the persons themselves to make decisions about what they want to do about the abuse. Be sure to inform them of professional services available in your community.

If the group member mentions abuse of a minor child, guidelines for protection of minors come into play. There are very strict laws governing the reporting of child abuse to the legal authorities. However, there are limitations under the seal of the confessional for clergy. Make sure that you talk about these issues with your pastor or priest.

Help for severe problems

If you recognize people with severe problems in your group, intervention may be warranted. At the first session, you can invite group members to talk with you if they feel they need more intensive help with the issues that come up. By doing this, members will not feel singled out.

Ahead of time, talk with your pastor or health care professionals. Most counties have mental health centers which are listed in the telephone book. There is usually a chapter of the mental health association of the state that offers resources, as well as county resources listed in books such as "First Call for Help." Shall we add publishing information? Some possible sources include local crisis hot lines, local county social service departments, county child and adult protection agencies, Lutheran Social Service, Catholic Social Services, and Jewish Social Services (most religious groups have social services available through their specific denomination), and legal aid.

Goals

The two main goals of this support and recovery group on self-esteem are to help the participants:

- Learn about themselves, each other, ways to improve their self-esteem, and their faith
- Grow and change as they share ideas, hear others, and receive emotional support from other group members.

In general, people attend support and recovery groups:

- To gain knowledge and insight about the topic
- To find new ways to enhance how they function in their lives
- To gain support from other people
- To gather ideas for change in their lives
- To meet new people
- To share ideas with people who have the same interest

The facilitator

The roles of the facilitator include:

- *Convener* (arranging the room appropriately, starting and ending the meeting on time)
- *Host* (providing refreshments before, during, and after the session—or coordinating others to do so)
- *Facilitator* (encouraging discussion and getting the most from the materials
- *Participant* (engaging in discussion and sharing your own growth experiences
- *Clean-up* (checking to see that the meeting room is left in the same or better condition as it was when the group entered)

Materials: Most sessions will be enhanced by the use of chalkboard and chalk or newsprint and markers (black or blue, not red). These will be used for recording group comments and ideas.

Using the chalkboard or newsprint to list items has the effect of making them group property. Always in view, the list often is an encouragement to participants to reflect on areas that otherwise might have eluded them.

Name tags will be useful in the first few sessions and possibly throughout the program.*

In terms of facilitating or leading this group, it is suggested that the facilitator have experienced being a member in some kind of support or recovery group. Then he or she will have a better idea of what to expect in a group setting.

Also, it is desirable that persons who serve as facilitators have some experience in group process and group dynamics. Leadership courses are offered through community education, by churches, at state universities or colleges, or in many other places.

You need to be able to keep the group moving and on track. This means you may have to take charge, give definite directives, and help the group get back to the subject once in a while. Practice being comfortable with the idea of taking charge.

Some people might linger for conversation after meetings. While that is helpful, the facilitator may need to suggest that they continue over a cup of coffee somewhere else. Courtesy to the host or consideration for the custodian might require that group members not stick around too long.*

* From Russell E. Fink and Barbara Owen-Fink, *Divorce: Survival and Hope* (Intersections Small Group Series), copyright © 1995 Augsburg Fortress.

A common problem

When a group member continually sidetracks the group, consider these actions:

- Make a ruling by group consensus that a person is not to talk for more than five minutes (or some other specific amount of time).

- When someone has overextended their time, make the time hand signal, or T-sign, by crossing the extended palm of one hand over the fingertips of the other hand.

- Give the person an advance warning when one minute remains and tell him or her to summarize quickly.

- Switch gears by telling the person, "Now we need to hear what some of the other members think. Thanks for your input."

If a person persistently interferes with group process, talk privately with him or her as soon as possible. Let the person know your concerns and ask if he or she sees a need for more in-depth therapy. If the person agrees, work with your pastor to help the person to find the best resource from the agencies available locally.

Special concerns related to the six sessions

Although some might think that a self-esteem group would be light and joyful, the reality is that nearly everyone's self-esteem has been wounded. Looking at the wounds and negative experiences of the past can be painful. In our culture, certain groups, among them women and people of color, have not been as valued and therefore have suffered more damage. In addition to the particular situations described below, be sensitive to what has happened to some people simply because they live in the culture they do.

Session 1: In the exercise under the first "Discovery" section, "Where It All Began," some people who were raised in dysfunctional or abusive families may remember very stressful times. Help them use their memories as starting points, but encourage them to move in positive directions. If the problems are severe, suggest that they talk with their pastor or physician about a referral to a therapist.

Session 2: Some might feel depressed about whatever problem they identify (workaholism, perfectionism, and so forth) in the third "Discovery" section, "Working on Problems that Hold Us Back." Again, encourage them to move on and plan some ways to do something about their identified problem.

Session 3: With the emphasis on families, those from families with severe problems such as violent or abusive behavior or alcoholism may have a hard time. Notice that the session includes close friends other than family, and some might feel closer to non-family people who have been supportive, perhaps their sponsor in AA, church friends, or members of other groups. Keep the focus broad enough so that the difficult family situations that some have won't prevent them from identifying relationships that have helped them.

Session 4: Discriminatory practices and harassment in social settings such as private clubs, schools, and communities may have significant impact on self-esteem. If group members talk about concerns with harassment at work, they need to be advised about reporting their concerns to the human resource department in their workplace.

Some who have experienced discrimination or harassment at work (women, people of color) may be angry and frustrated. The group can help them think of actions they can take and ways to rebuild their self-esteem.

Session 5: The second "Discovery" section, "When Our Appearance Changes," may be difficult for many, including those who have been in accidents, had cancer (perhaps hair loss, or surgical removal of tissue or body parts), live with disabilities, or are sensitive about aging. If you have questions about how a person is feeling, do not be afraid to ask him or her. The group can practice affirmations of each other and together can explore ways to live with less-than-ideal situations.

Be sensitive to the powerful feelings that can be associated with body-image. One suicide victim killed herself because she perceived she was aging and had bags under her eyes. She simply could not hear other people's assurances that she still was attractive. Negative thinking about appearance can mask a serious suicidal depression.

Session 6: Some may struggle with some of the material under the second "Discovery" section, "The Need for Balance." The goal is not to be perfect, but to be able to take small steps and make some changes (writing goals under "Goals and Dreams"). Group support is vital here.

Contents of this course

The movement in this course has a circular pattern. The beginning sessions look closely at who we are and what God says, then the course ventures out to our families, work and social contacts, culture, and world, and then back again to ourselves, what God says, and our dreams and hopes. The six sessions for this course on self-esteem are:

1. "Loving and Being Loved." Definitions of self-esteem; the Bible's words on loving ourselves, others, and God; and how we can nourish our self-esteem.

2. "Knowing and Accepting Myself." How God sees us, how we see ourselves, and finding ways to do something about problems that hold us back.

3. "Families and Friends." Our closest relationships, the life cycle, and the spiritual foundations we need to be able to love.

4. "The Wider World of Relationships." The importance of other people, the workplace and other social contacts, being "lights" in our worlds.

5. "The Matter of Appearance." Appreciating that our bodies are God-given, the image we have of our bodies, how changes in appearance affect us, what our culture tells us.

6. "Confidently on Our Way." Self-esteem is rooted in love, the need for balance, goals and dreams.

Facilitator helps for the six sessions

Each of the six chapters, or sessions, has three subthemes or sections. Each section is labeled "Discovery 1," "Discovery 2," or "Discovery 3." The suggestions that follow give some helps and elaborations for the material in them, but in general the best plan is to follow the sequence in the book, reading, discussing, and doing the exercises as they are presented. Suggestions on expanding the course beyond six questions are given below, on page 69.

At the beginning of each session, take time for one of the "Community Building" activities. Also check in briefly on how the group is doing, especially if it responds well to doing the stop-start activities. In that case, they need to report their progress at each meeting.

At the close of each session, choose a "Group Ministry Task" (or tasks) individuals are willing to do (suggestions are given for each session below), review the session briefly, share personal concerns and prayer concerns (these can be written down on page 74), and close with the printed prayer or other choices of prayers.

All through this course, the importance of support from the members for each other cannot be overemphasized. Only part of the work to increase our self-esteem can be done alone; much of it comes from the acceptance and love of others. Do all you can to set a positive, accepting, and supportive spirit among the group members.

1 Loving and Being Loved

Community Building

Plan to spend a little more time than usual for getting acquainted this first session, using both exercises if you wish. Also take time to set some beginning goals for the group and write them down (see page 73). They can be adjusted later if the group wants to adapt or enlarge them.

Discovery 1

Read and talk about the definitions of self-esteem, noting that self-esteem is related to other people. Read the Bible passage, noting that it assumes we love ourselves. Discuss self-love and how it differs from selfishness or self-centeredness.

Discovery 2

This may be a sensitive area for some (see above on page 64). Keep the discussion moving and encourage participants to include positive memories.

Discovery 3

Because the whole course is on this topic, this is just an introduction. Have the members write down their ideas for stop-start activities and see if they will agree to try one of each.

Wrap-up

Have everyone turn to page 10, noting the paragraphs about the "Group Ministry Task." Review with the group how outreach is integral to the session (see page 7 in the "Introduction"). Mention some possibilities and let the group choose one or more of them or think of their own ideas. Suggestions include: building others' self-esteem by phone calls, notes, or spoken compliments; teaching someone (perhaps a child) a skill that would enhance that person's self-image; sending cards to shut-ins; visiting people at a care center or hospital.

For closing, you might wish to add the Serenity Prayer (see page 16) to the closing prayer.

2 Knowing and Accepting Myself

Community Building

At the beginning, before or after the "Community Building" exercise, take time for the participants to tell how their "start-stop" activities went, and perhaps also their ministry tasks. They could meet in the same small groups as last time or do this as a total group.

The theme for this session is self-knowledge or self-perception. We often don't know as much about ourselves as we think, and sometimes we think we are bragging if we mention our good points. We need to acknowledge the good in ourselves and at the same time avoid grandiosity.

Discovery 1

The place to begin is the Bible. We are created by God, in God's image. God also knows that we are fallen creatures with many problems and weaknesses, but God loves us, redeemed us, and will stay with us to help us.

Discovery 2

Have the participants complete the three inventories and talk with each other about them. Work on some samples of affirmations together and encourage each person to try at least one the next week.

Discovery 3

If not all the problems listed are familiar to the participants, have them choose one that is. Then have them work on the exercise and talk with each other. Encourage them to identify some stop and start actions (ones they would feel good about) that relate to the problem they identified. Next week they can report their progress.

Wrap-up

The "Group Ministry Task" could be continuations of previous choices or perhaps add a new one, such as encouraging the church library to add books on self-esteem, or seeing if the group would like to purchase one or more self-esteem books for the library.

3 Families and Friends

Sessions 3 and 4 look at relationships; this time we look at those closest to us.

Community Building

As in previous sessions, the group can choose either the main exercise or the option, both on page 27.

Discovery 1

Use the visualization exercise to help everyone recall something about self-esteem issues at home. The purpose is to help them see both the helpful and unhelpful factors in their home situations that affected their self-esteem.

Discovery 2

This brief overview does not include great detail, but the group might want to focus on points where some members express the most interest, such as parenting, adolescence, or the older years.

Discovery 3

Our spiritual foundations have a lot to do with our ability to love ourselves and to relate to others. Invite the participants to tell what has helped them, and also how they would like to grow. Trying some new or expanded spiritual practices might be helpful.

Wrap-up

For the "Group Ministry Task," consider some action that would help others, perhaps bringing food next time for a food shelf or participating with a group or agency that helps people. Previously chosen tasks can also be continued.

4 The Wider World of Relationships

This session expands to relationships beyond those mentioned in Session 3 (closer relationships such as family).

Community Building

Do either the thought-starter exercise or the option, which can show participants some of the ways certain words build up or pull down our self-esteem.

Discovery 1

Help the participants realize how other people are mirrors to them. Our many-faceted interdependence is part of God's design. We need other people; they need us. By now the group may see how members are helping each other with some of the difficult issues.

Discovery 2

This section talks about work, but goes beyond to include volunteer activities, school, church, social clubs, and related groups. Discussion may touch on hard issues such as harassment and discrimination which likely have a significant impact on self-esteem.

Discovery 3

The third section lifts the participants' sights to the larger picture and what God may be calling them to be and do. Invite them to tell personal stories about themselves or people they know.

Wrap-up

One possible "Group Ministry Task" could be to plan an informal time, perhaps a coffee hour, with the church's teachers (Sunday school and other) to talk together about helping their students increase their self-esteem. Another task might be to find ways to tell those working in the church, paid or volunteer, how much their work is appreciated.

5 The Matter of Appearance

The way people perceive their physical selves is a very large component of self-esteem. Self-perception is changeable. For example, if we feel really good about ourselves, we don't care what we wear, how we look, or if our hair is messy. Nothing will get us down because we just plain feel good. There are those other times when the opposite is true.

Community Building

For the "Community Building" activity, think of past or current political figures, movie or entertainment celebrities, and others whose names have appeared in the news. Some possible names are Albert Einstein, Martin Luther King, Jr., Madonna, Prince, Mother Teresa, Florence Nightingale, George Washington Carver, and Abraham Lincoln. Quite likely verbal clues will be needed.

Discovery 1

Enjoy this section together, spending time on Psalms 8 and 139.

Discovery 2

This will be the most serious part of your discussion. Draw on the examples given but have the participants tell about their own experiences and ones they have read or heard about. Grieving over changes is to be expected, but with God's help, we can finally reach a sense of acceptance and peace.

Discovery 3

Extra activities here could include surveying what TV tells us is beautiful, or bringing magazines and looking through them. In the exercise when the participants think of someone whom they admire who is not a beauty, they will be reminded again that other characteristics matters much more than our current ideas of physical beauty.

Wrap-up

The "Group Ministry Task" can continue the theme of helping others with their self-esteem. Stop and start activities could be created in regard to family members or close friends; *stop* doing so much criticizing or fault finding, *start* thanking your children, your spouse, your friends for things they do.

6 Confidently on Our Way

This last session sums up some of the key ideas in the course, looks at balance, and helps the participants think of ways to continue to build their self-esteem.

Community Building

Both "Community Building" activities give participants a chance to reflect on their experience with the course, and to tell other group members what their experience has been.

Discovery 1

This section looks again at loving ourselves, loving others, and loving God.

Discovery 2

The first exercise gives a sampling from many areas of life: social, spiritual, financial, physical, emotional, and several others. It helps everyone look at well-being in general because that helps self-esteem. The second exercise provides a way to find the healthy balance in regard to some of the issues raised in earlier sessions.

Discovery 3

Several suggestions are given here. They include a twenty-one day experiment, as well as the use of a "force field analysis" for a specific goal. Help the participants review the main themes and strategies, and encourage them to continue those that they choose to do.

Wrap-up

Include discussion of ways for the group members to continue group ministry activities, if they wish.

How to expand the course beyond six sessions

Because each of the six sessions has three "Discovery" sections, a course of eighteen sessions is a possibility, although the "Discovery" sections do vary in amount of content and time needed for each. Here are some suggestions for dividing each session, thereby making more sessions possible.

Session 1 lends itself to division into two or three sessions, using the first two "Discovery" sections for one, and the ideas on nourishing our self-esteem for the second session.

Session 2 could also be two or three sessions. The second and third "Discovery" sections could easily stand alone, giving everyone more time for the inventories and identified problem areas.

For each of the "Discovery" sections, the group member could do some homework. When they are working on their inventories, they could ask their family members and friends how those people perceive their gifts and talents. For the identified problem areas, they could choose more than one, and do more homework about where those problems began (childhood, adolescence). They could also talk to others who say they have the same difficulty.

Session 3, which is on families, friends, and the life cycle, could become three sessions. For the first "Discovery" section, discussions about how family members relate to each other and how those interactions impact family members' self-esteem could be emphasized more. Some research could be done about what happens when families are abusive or otherwise dysfunctional.

For the second "Discovery" section, the group could spend more time on the stages of the life cycle and also on parenting. Some might want to spend more time on adolescence and young adulthood, both their own and their children's. That is the time when people are most influenced by their peer relationships. Some might be interested in looking at the later adult years. Perhaps a social worker could be a guest speaker and focus on children, adolescents, or the elderly.

The third "Discovery" section is on spiritual foundations and could prove to be an uplifting and informative session by itself.

Session 4 moves to the wider world of relationships, including work, and could probably become two sessions, one using the first and third "Discovery" sections and the other using the second "Discovery" section. For the latter, the group can explore how the money from our jobs impacts our sense of worth, but also the importance of feeling valued as a person at work and in other social settings.

Session 5, which is on how we regard our bodies and the impact of body changes, could be three or four sessions. Each of the themes in the "Discovery" sections can easily be expanded. For the first "Discovery" section, a pastor could be a guest speaker. For the second, more time can be taken telling personal experiences; guests such as counselors and physical therapists could add their insights. The third "Discovery" section could even be two sessions; one for discussing the topic and how it affects us, another for seeing a movie where physical attractiveness is a key, looking through magazines, or watching television or video clips.

Session 6, "Confidently on Our Way," might be two sessions. Have a separate session on the second "Discovery" section and combine the other two. The one on "The Need for Balance" would be an excellent time to discuss the impact of humor and acceptance of self. We will never be perfect, and it is fun to enjoy ourselves and each other just the way we are.

The last session could be on personal dreams and goal setting. It can include discussion of how we can practice acceptance of ourselves as fallible human beings, yet move ahead as we are able. The Serenity Prayer (page 16) can be reviewed again. We do not venture out alone; God is always with us, guiding us.

How to adapt the course to a retreat format

This course would work well as the basis of a retreat, but choices would need to be made among the "Discovery" sections in each session. Here is a possible schedule for a Friday night through Sunday noon retreat.

Friday night

Session 1: Do all three "Discovery" sections (but only briefly introduce stop-start actions).

Saturday morning

Session 2: Give some attention to all three "Discovery" sections, shortening as needed.

Saturday afternoon

Session 5: Go through the material on self-esteem and bodies. Then go out for recreation and enjoy your bodies!

Saturday evening

Use the first "Discovery" section of Session 3, "Our Closest Relationships," along with the first "Discovery" section of Session 4, "Our Wider Friendships." Close with worship using ideas from the third "Discovery" sections of Session 3, "Loving God and Others" and Session 4, "Called to Be Lights."

Sunday morning

Use all three "Discovery" sections of Session 6, shortening as needed, but use ideas from the first, "It's about Love," for a closing worship service.

Appendix

Group directory

Record information about group members here.

Names	Addresses	Phone Numbers

Group commitments

"Do not be conformed to this world, but be transformed by the renewing of your minds, so that you may discern what is the will of God—what is good and acceptable and perfect" (Romans 12:2).

- For our time together, we have made the following commitments to each other

- Goals for our study of this topic are

- Our group ministry tasks are

- My personal action plan is

Prayer requests

Prayers

■ Closing Prayer

Lord God, you have called your servants to ventures of which we cannot see the ending, by paths as yet untrodden, through perils unknown. Give us faith to go out with good courage, not knowing where we go, but only that your hand is leading us and your love supporting us; through Jesus Christ our Lord. Amen.

Lutheran Book of Worship, copyright 1978, 153

■ The Lord's Prayer

(If you plan to use the Lord's Prayer, record the version your group uses in the next column.)

Resources

Books

Many of these titles are cited by the writers of this resource.

Bradshaw, John. *Creating Love: The Next Great Stage of Growth.* N.Y.: Bantam Books, 1993. Insights on how to work to create healthy relationships with families, friends, ourselves, and God.

Briggs, Dorothy Corkville. *Your Child's Self-Esteem: The Key to His Life.* N.Y.: Doubleday, 1975. Helps parents know how to create strong feelings of self-worth in their children.

Christgau, John. *Sierra Sue II: The Story of a P-51.* San Mateo, Calif.: Great Planes Press, 1994. An in-depth account of a man's fortitude and courage in overcoming physical disability.

Clarke, Jean Illsley. *Self-Esteem: A Family Affair.* San Francisco: HarperSanFrancisco, 1985. An excellent book filled with creative ways to improve self-esteem in families, especially young teens and children.

Clarke, Jean Illsey and Connie Dawson. *Growing Up Again: Parenting Ourselves, Parenting Our Children.* Minneapolis: Hazelden, 1989. Helps for those who experienced poor parenting and want to change their own parenting skills.

DeGrote-Sorensen, Barbara, and David Allen Sorensen. *'Tis a Gift to Be Simple.* Minneapolis: Augsburg, 1992. Shows how people can feel better about themselves through making one's lifestyle simpler and healthier.

Ellis, Albert, and Robert A. Harper. *A New Guide to Rational Living.* North Hollywood, Calif.: Wilshire Books, 1975.

Larsen, Earnie. *What Do I Believe About Myself? Building Self-Esteem in a Negative World.* Brooklyn Park, Minn.: E. Larsen Enterprises, Inc., 1988. Six pamphlets giving practical steps for learning to like ourselves.

Larsen, Earnie. *Stage II Recovery: Life Beyond Addiction.* San Francisco: Harper & Row, 1985. A practical guide on how to identify and change self-defeating behavior.

McGinnis, Alan Loy. *Confidence: How to Succeed at Being Yourself.* Minneapolis: Augsburg, 1987. Practical helps for increasing self-confidence and appreciating personal worth.

Palladino, Connie. *Developing Self-Esteem: A Positive Guide for Personal Success.* Los Altos, Calif.: Crisp Publications, 1989. Practical helps and exercises to learn about yourself and appreciate your worth.

Pelkey, Eddie Jane Gavin. *Gifts of the Heart.* Nashville, Tenn.: Winston-Derek, 1992. The story of a young woman's emotional and spiritual growth.

Powell, John. *The Secret of Staying in Love.* Niles, Ill.: Argus, 1974. Shows how the key to relationships with others is a genuine acceptance of self. (Out of print.)

Movies

Many movies deal with a variety of issues related to self-esteem, and are easily rented from a video store. Here are just a few.

Grumpy Old Men

The Breakfast Club

Clean and Sober

Fried Green Tomatoes

Interiors

Television

Several current shows, especially those about people in recovery or dealing with difficult situations in life, can be watched with an eye to what they say about self-esteem. Observe what they show about the ways different characters feel about their own worth and what they are doing to help their self-esteem. Here are some examples.

"The John Larroquette Show"

"Northern Exposure"

"Sisters"

"Grace Under Fire"

Please check the INTERSECTIONS book you are evaluating.

- ☐ Following Jesus
- ☐ The Bible and Life
- ☐ Captive and Free
- ☐ Caring and Community
- ☐ Death and Grief
- ☐ Divorce
- ☐ Faith
- ☐ Jesus: Divine and Human
- ☐ Men and Women
- ☐ Peace
- ☐ Praying
- ☐ Self-Esteem

Please tell us about your small group.

1. Our group had an average attendance of ____.

2. Our group was made up of
   ____ Young adults (19-25 years)
   ____ Adults (most between 25-45 years)
   ____ Adults (most between 45-60 years)
   ____ Adults (most between 60-75 years)
   ____ Adults (most 75 and over)
   ____ Adults (wide mix of ages)
   ____ Men (number) and ____ women (number)

3. Our group (answer as many as apply)
   ____ came together for the sole purpose of studying this INTERSECTIONS book.
   ____ has decided to study another INTERSECTIONS book.
   ____ is an ongoing Sunday school group.
   ____ met at a time other than Sunday morning.
   ____ had only one facilitator for this study.

---FOLD CARD IN HERE, SEAL WITH TAPE, AND MAIL TODAY!---

Please tell us about your experience with INTERSECTIONS.

4. What I like best about my INTERSECTIONS experience is

5. Three things I want to see the same in future INTERSECTIONS books are

6. Three things I might change in future INTERSECTIONS books are

7. Topics I would like developed for new INTERSECTIONS books are

8. Our group had ____ sessions for the six chapters of this book.

9. Other comments I have about INTERSECTIONS are

Thank you for taking the time to fill out and return this questionnaire.

NO POSTAGE
NECESSARY
IF MAILED
IN THE
UNITED STATES

BUSINESS REPLY MAIL
FIRST-CLASS MAIL   PERMIT NO. 22120   MINNEAPOLIS, MN

POSTAGE WILL BE PAID BY ADDRESSEE

Augsburg Fortress
ATTN INTERSECTIONS TEAM
PO BOX 1209
MINNEAPOLIS MN 55440-8807